POPE FRANCIS,
Conscience of the World:
Building Needed Bridges in a Troubled World

by

John Raymaker

and Gerald Grudzen

Hamilton Books
Lanham • Boulder • New York • London

Published by Hamilton Books
4501 Forbes Boulevard, Suite 200, Lanham, Maryland 20706
www.rowman.com

6 Tinworth Street, London SE11 5AL, United Kingdom

Copyright © 2020 by The Rowman & Littlefield Publishing Group, Inc.

All rights reserved. No part of this book may be reproduced in any form or by any electronic or mechanical means, including information storage and retrieval systems, without written permission from the publisher, except by a reviewer who may quote passages in a review.

British Library Cataloging in Publication Information Available

ISBN 978-0-7618-7192-7 (pbk.: alk. paper)
ISBN 978-0-7618-7193-4 (e-book)

CONTENTS

Foreword
v

Introduction
vii

PART ONE
Rebuilding the Earth and the Church
on the Model of Prophetic Visionaries

Chapter 1
Building New Foundational-Missionary Bridges in a Divided World
3

Chapter 2
How Pope Francis Has Given New Foci to the Church's Mission
21

Chapter 3
Pierre Teilhard de Chardin (1881-1955) and
Pope Francis: Catholic Visionaries
33

PART TWO
The Transformative Roles of Religion
Across the Planet

Chapter 4
Transitional Glocal Issues
49

Chapter 5
Pope Francis's Glocal Engagements with the Middle East and Africa
73

Chapter 6
The Church in Latin America
85

Chapter 7
Compassionate Ways to Heal and Create in Asia
95

PART THREE
Pioneering Effective Christian Ministries in a Divided, Conflicted World

Chapter 8
New Forms of Community and Ministries in the Age of Pope Francis
105

Chapter 9
A Global but Divided Christianity
Needs Glocal Initiatives to Cope with the Future
119

Selected Bibliography
137

Index
141

FOREWORD

This book shows with great skill how Pope Francis—the first non-European Pope since 741—is concerned with far more than the Catholic Church. Described as a great prophet and bridge-builder rather than someone who builds dividing walls, his heart, words, and actions show compassion and love for the whole of humanity and its common home, the Earth. Here the local and global are intimately interwoven, new paths are needed and tried, greatly to the annoyance of traditional Catholic reactionaries. Like his Jesuit predecessor, Pierre Teilhard de Chardin, Pope Francis is seen as belonging to those Catholic visionaries who are deeply concerned with the great ethical and spiritual challenges of our contemporary world, much in need of new forms of Christian ministry and community as well as more collaboration between people of different faiths. Readers will benefit greatly from the examples given of Pope Francis's engagement with the variety of people, cultures, and religions in different parts of the world. This book should be widely read and discussed. It can help to inspire more understanding and collaboration between different parts of humanity and make us realize that we all belong to the same Earth and Humanity and must work together to ensure the future of our common home.

—Ursula King
*Professor Emerita of Theology and Religious Studies,
University of Bristol, England*

INTRODUCTION

We argue in this book that Pope Francis has a "glocal worldview."[1] Chapter 1 begins with a quote from Rachel Carson who prophetically addressed environmental issues in the 1950's. Such issues have been one of Francis' major concerns as shown in his Encyclical *Laudato Si* ("On Care for our Common Home"). *Laudato Si* urges all humans help save the planet. We argue that the pope's breakthrough-efforts can best be approached from a comprehensive, glocal viewpoint. To put this in perspective, let us note that the pope is superficially accused by some of not sufficiently adhering to Church's "Tradition," of being a "rebel" who rejects the Church's tradition as it were. On the contrary, far from rebelling, his theology "flows out of *Dei Verbum*, the Second Vatican Council's "Dogmatic Constitution on Divine Revelation", which he develops in rejuvenating ways. He looks at Tradition through the lens of evangelization."[2] He does reflect on key themes such as embracing newness and being open to conversion. He does tend to "surprise" us as when he links climate change with poverty, indigenous rights and social justice issues. His many concerns for the good of all are punctuated with his infectious smiles which energize people, especially the young. Wim Wender's film on the pope, *A Man of his Word* depicts St. Francis' conversion and the vision he had of rebuilding God's Church. Rebuilding the Church and caring for the earth are part of the pope's mission. His encyclical *Laudato Si* takes its name from St. Francis' *Canticle*.[3] Like his namesake, his idea of "success"[4] is to gently care for all. Rebuilding the Church is dramatically symbolized in the determination[5] to rebuild the Notre Dame Cathedral in Paris after the disastrous fire of April, 2019. Construction on the Cathedral began in 1163–18 years before St. Francis' birth. Times have changed but the goal of rebuilding the Church is an unending task, one for which our charismatic pope is well suited. This was abundantly clear in his visit at the World Youth Day in Panama (January 2019) where, he talked to young people in their own idiom. They reciprocated enthusiastically—realizing that this man wants to share with them both the joys and demands of life. With the pope, we are concerned with the injunction Jesus gave the Church to preach the Good News to all nations.

For Stephen Bevans and Roger Schroeder, the Church's mission is a "prophetic dialogue," a phrasing we build on.[6] As did Pope John XXIII, Pope Francis speaks from the heart. Both pontiffs reached back into the Middles Ages when choosing their papal name with a view to blend the traditional and modern realities of the Catholic Church. This requires renewing, reforming the church. James Carroll asks whether the cardinals who elected Francis pope in 2013 knew what they were getting. "Francis has spoken forcefully and forthrightly about the world's most urgent problems—the bankruptcy of free-market capitalism, the plight of migrants, . . . climate change, demagogic populism, economic inequality. He has done all this with verve, good humor, and a self-accepting modesty. And, most important, he has been heard. The dangerous currents of world politics have made him into a global tribune of human aspiration; it is no longer news that the pope is a true Christian,"[7] the conscience of the world.[8] Some unjustly criticize Pope Francis for deviating from tradition. We focus on how he is glocally integrating today's new realities from ethical-theological-spiritual perspectives within traditional Catholic teachings in need of updating. In a world full of uncertainties, Pope Francis has found a sure touch to pinpoint where adjustments should be made to restore a new equilibrium across a vast spectrum of ecclesial and political issues.

Notes

1 "Glocal," a portmanteau of global and local, points to the simultaneous universalizing and particularizing tendencies in contemporary life. We are now told that before long, companies will need to think and act globally while servicing customers locally. The term "globalization" is often used to suggest a dichotomy, even a radical disassociation, between the "global" (multinational corporations, international terrorism, the entertainment industry) and "the local" (neighborhood, town, ethnicity, etc.). We use "glocalization" to denote the dynamic relationships between these two realms while pointing to their mutually reinforcing aspects. See also https://leipglo.com/about-us/ The pope insists that the only sustainable future for a global world is one in which people help foster a globalization of solidarity in an uncertain world. Researchers have found that there are close links between local climate and the occurrence of severe, threatening diseases in other parts of the

world. See http://climate.org/archive/topics/health.html Such events illustrate why a glocal-ethical theology is needed.

On "A Glocal Theology in the Pope Francis Era," see www.kings.uwo.ca/kings/assets/File/academics/centres/ carct/Glocal-Theology.pdf which samples glocal theologies developed in Canada. Many authors we quote in our text favor glocal worldviews. They write about possible repercussions of the actions of individuals or organizations upon others at home or abroad: crimes against humanity or persons must *not* be ignored.

2 John Dool, "Dei Verbum, Pope Francis and the Ongoing Renewal of Tradition" is a perspective on glocal theologies. For the glocal aspects of the Bible, see *Transforming Graduate Biblical Education: Ethos and Discipline*, edited by Elisabeth Schussler Fiorenza and Kent Harold Richards (Atlanta: Society of Biblical Literature, 2010) 55-58.

3 St. Francis of Assisi's Canticle of the Sun praises God for creating Brother Sun, Sister Moon and all creatures.

4 "Success" at www.success.com/4-leadership-lessons-from-pope-francis holds up the pope's leadership abilities.

5 The outpouring of support for rebuilding Notre Dame symbolizes humanity's yearning for transcendence. Great art and architecture can express and even incarnate this yearning such as we find expressed in Notre Dame. With the pope we explore the Middle Ages' gift to our modern era that has lost much of its sense of transcendence.

6 Stephen B. Bevans and Roger P. Schroeder, *Prophetic Dialogue*, New York, Orbis, 2011. In our view, prophetic dialogue furthers Hans Kung's Global Ethic project to help different cultures live together in constructive ways.

7 James Carroll, "Two Scenes from Pope Francis's Revolution of Tenderness," May 1, 2017. www.newyorker.com/news/news-desk/two-scenes-from-pope-franciss-revolution-of-tenderness   Quoting Bruno Giussani, Carroll adds: "Francis has become possibly the only moral voice capable of reaching people across boundaries and providing clarity and a compelling message of hope."

8 Conscience is an inner feeling or voice viewed as acting as a guide to the rightness or wrongness of one's behavior. The film, A Man of his Word, testifies to Pope Francis being the conscience of the world through his habit of pointing to his hearers the sense of right and wrong in human conduct and how they might remedy problems.

PART ONE
Rebuilding the Earth and the Church on the Model of Prophetic Visionaries

CHAPTER 1

Building New Foundational-Missionary Bridges in a Divided World

Rachel Carson's *Silent Spring* (1962) laid the foundations for the environmental movement. In the dedication of her history-making book to Albert Schweitzer, she quotes him:

> *"Man has lost the capacity to foresee and to forestall. He will end by destroying the earth."*

Our book argues that Pope Francis has spent his life building bridges. As priest and bishop, he *foresaw* situations in need of change. Since being elected pope, he has urged humanity to help *forestall* climate crises. He has reached deeply into our psyches, even our souls through his contagious charisma. The world needs charismatic, down-to-earth leaders such as Pope Francis. As the son of middle-class Italian immigrants, Cardinal Bergoglio had denied himself the luxuries that previous archbishops in Buenos Aires had enjoyed. In October 2012, six months before becoming pope, it was under his leadership that Argentina's bishops issued a collective apology for the church's failures to protect its flock by remaining silent during the post-1976 military dictatorship. As pope, he has made it clear that he considers social outreach, rather than doctrinal battles, to be the Church's main task today. We shall often refer to his encyclical *Laudato Si*, and his two apostolic exhortations, *Evangelii Gaudium* (*Joy of the Gospel*), and *Gaudete et Exsultate* (*Rejoice and Be Glad*) which have set the tone for his papacy. *Joy of the Gospel* is the document upon which conservative Catholics have zeroed in to attack what they take to be the pope's quasi-heretical teaching. They fail to see that joy is intrinsic to Jesus' Good News. Young people need joy in their lives as they face an uncertain future. That is why they react to him so favorably. The pope emphasizes that his *Joy of the Gospel*, ends with a spirituality of mission so as to reinforce *Laudato Si*.[1] This spirituality consistently distinguishes between superficial kinds of entertainment to be rejected and sound notions of a healthy cultural leisure.

David Gray has examined the pope's Christology on the basis of his 2013-2014 homilies. He concludes that the pope stresses Christian ideals. In his homilies, Francis keeps reminding us that we encounter Jesus through Christian living. Gray compares the message of Pope Francis with that of Schweitzer's rejection of liberal theology in his famous *The Quest of the Historical Jesus* (1906). In *Quest*, Schweitzer insists that we should not understand Jesus' teaching on the Kingdom of God as a *mere inward*, spiritual reality. Rather, Jesus speaks of a seed which has to grow in our hearts. The goal of history is to help bring about God's Kingdom.[2] We cannot do so on our own because the Kingdom transcends history. It can only be initiated by God himself. Still, we humans do have an indispensable role to play. Schweitzer spent his life serving God through his fellow human beings. He died in 1965 at the age of 90 in Africa after 50 years of serving patients as a medical missionary. Schweitzer was a multitalented man, a genius, a prophet for the modern age who not only warned humanity of impending dangers but took the steps he could to help avoid the catastrophes humans now face due to their shortsighted loss of religious-Christian values. Gray argues that, like Schweitzer, Pope Francis knows what "journeying with Christ" means. Schweitzer focused on the failure of many Christians to truly follow Christ. Pope Francis, for his part, has kept reminding us, beginning with his very first papal homily, that "When we journey without the Cross, when we build without the Cross, when we profess Christ without the Cross, we are not disciples of the Lord, we are worldly: we may be bishops, priests, cardinals, popes, but not disciples of the Lord."[3] The Vatican II Council (1962-1965)[4] closed the year Schweitzer died. Rachel Carson, Schweitzer, and Pope Francis have all been bridge builders. Their far-sighted visionary actions are models for building needed bridges in a divided world.[5] The present text argues that Pope Francis' "glocally-ethical" views on the many challenges facing humanity converge in appropriately harmonious ways.

Building Glocal Bridges in a Digitalized-but-Divided World

Pontifex (or "Pontiff") means "bridge-builder." "Supreme Pontiff" is one of the pope's official titles. It derives from the pre-Christian religions of Rome. It was used to refer to the highest office in Rome's polytheistic religion. After the death of a member of the second Triumvirate who had held the title of *Pontifex Maximus*, the mighty Emperor Augustus assumed the title for himself to strengthen his position as ruler of Rome. The title helped successive Roman emperors consolidate their authority. Even after the Emperor Constantine made Christianity the Empire's official religion, he retained the office of *Pontifex Maximus*. It was under this title that he convened the first Church Council at Nicaea in 325 AD.[6]

It was not until the Empire split in two, with the Western Empire going to the pious, youthful Emperor Gratian (359-383) that the pope was first called *Pontifex Maximus*. Influenced, by St. Ambrose, Gratian did not feel that it was right for him to bear this title for he was not even a Christian priest. This is why, in 380, he bestowed the title upon Damasus I, the first Pope to be called *Pontifex Maximus*—"supreme bridge-builder."[7] We argue that Pope Francis is transforming the traditional papal role of Supreme Pontiff as he builds "revolutionary," glocal bridges. He is gentle—yet firm in rebuking clerics who have betrayed Gospel priorities. By way of conscienticizing Christians of good will, he asks them to live simply as did Jesus—as exemplified in the Good News of St. Matthew's Gospel where we read e. g.:

> Matt 6:19—Do not store up for yourselves treasures on earth, where moths and vermin destroy; and where thieves break in and steal. For where your treasure is, there your heart will also be.
> Matt 6:24—No one can serve two masters. Either you will hate the one and love the other, or you will be devoted to the one and despise the other. You cannot serve both God and money.

As the first non-European pope since 741, Pope Francis has focused on authentic values in an age discontinuous with the past. His *Laudato Si* stresses the need to reduce emissions of carbon dioxide and other highly polluting gases. He has opted against the pomp and circumstance that characterized the papacy up until Vatican II. Pope John XXIII had begun to instill a new spirit of collaborative renewal in the Church—one that eventually culminated in Bergoglio's election as pope in 2013. He decided not to live in the Papal Palace. He began to live "a normal life," he says, in a modest Vatican "hotel." He wants to be an efficient bridge-builder—one with a caring heart. We shall concentrate on Pope Francis' way of bridge-building by focusing on vital issues threatening the world. As Jesus, the prophets of old, Albert Schweitzer and Rachel Carson have warned, we today must act responsibly. The encroachments of capitalism, today's complex technologies and instant communication that enable corporations to avoid paying taxes, etc, all suggest that the Church must help society change course. In that spirit, we set out to build glocally-spiritual bridges in a divided-divisive world. Our attempts to bridge issues confronting humanity today take account of many key factors—both historical and present—affecting Catholic ideals:

- one's inner self and "outer" self. Creative people may have several inner selves—not to confused with split personalities.[8] Thomas Merton, for instance has helped people find their true, spiritual self. It is a matter of reaching deep into the human psyche and types of spiritualities that can ground the reaching.
- The various ways of living a life of holiness. John Berchmans, a Jesuit novice who died in 1621 at the age of 22 had as his motto *Age quod agis* ("Do well what you are actually doing"). One of the mottos of St. Bernard of Clairvaux and of St. Aloysius Gonzaga was "How does that matter to eternity?" These two mottos complement one another. The latter is foundational, the former invites us to live fruitfully. One is to be "selfless" in life so as to offset false beliefs about reality—as is also taught, e. g., in Zen Buddhism.
- The evolving sense of consciousness among men and women in the age of *me-too. Feminists have come a long way in assuming leadership in many areas of life, including religion and the Church.[9]
- Celibacy and sexual abuse scandals that have rocked the Church and led to much soul-searching.[10]

Humans can be ruthless. Because of this, with Pope Francis, we seek to build glocal bridges of mercy. An irony of Christian history is that Jesus in the gospels repeatedly urges us to seek the Kingdom of God; in fact, there are not enough active takers. Jesus's message in his Good Samaritan parable (Luke 10:25-37) is clear: "Love your enemies, do good to those who hate you, bless those who curse you, pray for those who abuse you. If anyone strikes you on the cheek, offer the other also; and from anyone who takes away your coat do not withhold even your shirt. (Luke 6:27-29). It certainly is not easy to live as a true Christian in a secularized age when the Church is being pushed to the margins. Few young people are now given a thorough Christian education. In view of today's problems and challenges, let us recall the distinction the Vatican II Council made between the *internal* mission of the Church (educating believers, reaching out toward a dechristianized West) and the Church's mission to the external world. The latter refers to the traditional missionary endeavors to bring the Gospel to the non-baptized as well as the Church's outreach to non-Christian religions.[11] Pope Francis has taken initiatives on all these fronts. In the face of today's "tough" missionary realities, we seek to expand the notion of mission as prophetic dialogue by emphasizing some of the bridge-building aspects of the Church's overall mission. We do so by stressing the importance of a glocal consciousness. The Church has long been a glocal institution as is evident in the traditional *Urbi et Orbi* papal blessings given to the city of Rome and to the entire world.

Mission as Prophetic Dialogue Based on a Sound Cultural Anthropology

In 2004, Stephen B. Bevans and Roger P. Schroeder published *Constants in Context: A Theology of Mission for Today*. It compares three historical types of approaches to the Church's mission from earliest times (100-301) to the 20th century. The first type conceived Christian missionary activity as participating in the very life of the Trinitarian God. "God is imaged as a missionary God, overflowing with love, mercy and healing for the created world."[12] A second type concentrates on Jesus' liberating vision of the Reign of God—the inauguration of which the church is called to join in. Thirdly, mission is understood in terms of the direct proclamation of Jesus the Christ as the unique savior of the world. None of the three approaches exclude the other two; each implies a particular way of doing missionary work. Each is a valid way to carry out the mission Jesus entrusted the Church as recorded in Matt 28:19-20; Mk 16:15-16; Lk 24:47-48; Jn 20-21; Acts1:8. The authors suggest that there is a need to "develop a way of speaking about mission that would include each of these contemporary approaches to mission in one single, dynamic concept that would serve to offer a creative synthesis or creative tension among them all." (Ibid). They stress that the modern focus on transformative liberation emerged within the early churches of Greater Syria—not in the Platonic outlook stemming from Alexandra at the beginning of the third century. The communities at or near Antioch emphasized the perfectibility of human nature based upon the example of Jesus reaching out to the outcasts and to the marginalized. But there coexisted a theology of the Church as the Body of Christ which challenged the prevailing social structures of the first century. The historical perspective of these early churches led them to proclaim that sin entered human history with Adam and Eve. "But, despite sin, God as Father and Shepherd continues mercifully to lead and guide humanity throughout history. God sent Jesus to free humanity from Satan's clutches and so to make possible continued growth, until at the End all will be Recapitulated in him."[13]

Bevans and Schroeder updated their *Context* book in 2011 with *Prophetic Dialogue* which identifies six elements inherent to Mission today: Witness and Proclamation, Liturgy, Prayer and Contemplation, the Integrity of Creation, Interreligious/Secular Dialogue, Inculturation and Reconciliation.[14] *Prophetic Dialogue* reflects John Paul II's teaching in *Redemptoris Missio* that "mission" must be understood as "a single, complex reality."[15] While it is true that proclaiming the gospel of Jesus has a certain "permanent priority" (*Redemptoris Missio*, 44), it is equally true that the words of proclamation" must be rooted in an authentic being of the church. The church must incarnate what it proclaims in the very fiber of its community life. It does so by participating in God's mission—radically dialogical as God is in God's self—and radically prophetic as is seen when God's Word speaks of hope, encouragement, challenge, and where need be, condemnation. Our aim is to update and extend Bevans and Schroeder's views by including the interfaith perspectives Pope Francis has stressed. The Church's ability to "incarnate" its message in the 21st century is challenged by the increasing secularization of western societies lacking adequate moral or spiritual foundations.[16] The media today focus on satisfying people's desires—not on promoting the common good. Firms such as Facebook and Google have evolved within a few years into giant mega-corporations that can monopolize their users' attention— giving them de facto control over the subliminal messages conveyed over digital technologies. Being dependent on advertising as they expand into new markets, they are concerned with the bottom line.[17] How reinstate adequate moral foundations? The Church has had less and less impact on the younger generation in the western world, but Catholic lay fraternities such as Sant' Egidio have flourished in developing countries with less pronounced secularized cultures. Integrating a sound cultural heritage through the use of technology is now a challenge facing the Church. In terms of today's global political and economic realities, personal and group conversions are needed if we are to promote the common good.[18] The Church must develop glocal spiritualities that resonate with the young. Pope Francis' initiatives respond to present needs. He is helping the Church adapt its traditions within a pluralistic, global setting that does not neglect technological realities. We stress small Christian communities as one crucial means of doing so.

Based on the pope's dedication to mercy,[19] we are undertaking a missionary bridge-building strategy that explores spiritualities and community life relevant to the present age. Just as Pope John XXIII opened a new chapter in the Church's life with Vatican Council II, so Pope Francis has been charting new ground for the Church. He knows that the Church must collaborate with other faith communities in promoting the common good. How do this—while tackling the many challenges posed by global climate change, poverty, racism, sexism, Islamophobia and isolationism? Finding glocal alternatives to the dark forces haunting modern culture requires that Catholics form partnerships with other faith groups which also face similar challenges. Modern prophets such as Mahatma Gandhi, Martin Luther King, Jr[20] Dorothy Day, Thomas Merton, and the Berrigan brothers all reached out to people of good will. They forged common bonds around commonly held values.

Pope Francis has invited not just Catholics but all people of good will to help save the planet for future generations. Young people have taken to the streets because they *are* worried. In view of a world threatened by moral relativism, we stress that a theology of mission should strive to bridge the gaps in the foundations of political, moral, and international life. We must find ways to transcend the moral relativism incarnated in a Donald Trump, a Xi in China, or an Erdogan in Turkey. Our premise is that each genuine Christian *should-be-and-can be* a bridge builder against the threats facing us. Nor should we let the media's self-promoting agenda victimize us. Our prophetic dialogue is based on a sound, glocal cultural anthropology— one aware of Christian Reus-Smit's warning that "International Relations Theory (IR Theory)" has failed to understand culture. IR's main schools cling to an outdated understanding of how civilizations work. They see "cultures as tightly integrated, neatly bounded, and clearly differentiated."[21] This view has been rejected by cultural anthropologists who see cultures as "heterogeneous and contradictory, highly porous, and deeply entwined and interrelated" entities. For Reus-Smit, IR theorists have misunderstood the roles of conflicting symbols and stories. They call themselves "realists"; in fact they frequently make arguments that rest on cultural assumptions. Reus-Smit cites Henry Kissinger's view that the erosion of our cultural foundation "poses a fundamental threat." Kissinger asks how can 'regions with such divergent cultures, histories, and traditional theories of order vindicate the legitimacy of any common system? For Reus-Smit, cultural anthropology is relevant when it explains how rational choices are made; when it accommodates cultural preferences; when it argues that common knowledge "is essential to solving coordination problems." (Ibid). IR fails on this latter point. We argue that Pope Francis has found the happy middle,[22] based on the glocal facts of actual and historical happenings.

The Ambiguous Legacies of the
Ages of Chivalry and Colonialism [23]

Many readers have been fascinated by Cervantes' story of Don Quixote. What is often missed in reading that story is that Cervantes was actually mourning the passing of Christian ideals at the beginning of the modern age. Don Quixote, obsessed with the chivalrous ideals touted in books he had read, decides to take up his lance and sword to defend the helpless and destroy the wicked. To him, the windmills simply look like the monsters that have destroyed his ideals and this must be undone.

For his part, Joseph Conrad interpreted ideals through the lenses of his being repulsed by colonialism. At the age of fifteen, Conrad, then known as Korzeniowski, was admonished by his tutor for being "an incorrigible, hopeless Don Quixote" just because he wanted to become a seaman. Conrad's *The Heart of Darkness* centers around Marlow,[24] an introspective riverboat captain, and his journey up the Congo River on his way to meet Kurtz, reputed to be a capable idealist. Marlow gradually realizes that Kurtz and his employers are brutal. The native inhabitants have been reduced to forced labor; they suffer terribly from overwork and ill treatment. The cruelty of the colonialist-imperial enterprise contrasts sharply with the impassive and majestic jungle surrounding the Belgian settlements, making them appear to be tiny islands amidst a vast darkness. The ambiguity in the novel is that Marlow wants us to understand his own story while shielding himself from blame. Conrad is a seer who reveals and veils the truth.[25]

The ambiguities of life keep on haunting those who would follow Christ who is the Way, the Truth and the Life (John 14: 6). Over the past centuries, many religious orders and congregations of men and women have recruited members to help them fully live by Christian ideals. As was the case with St. Benedict in his time, so today Christian life must be based on correctly assessing the human heart and societal needs, on building genuine communities based on Gospel ideals. Vatican II and modern popes have not been chasing windmills, nor have they surrendered to evil.[26] Evil will not overwhelm us if we do live the Good News. Our Chapter Eight examines the roles of small Christian communities that promote interpersonal dialogue and biblical reflection within a familial context. They complement the way parishes celebrate the liturgy. Being a Christian in a digital, depersonalized environment is helped by intimate, meditative forms of sharing—on the Beatitudes, for example. In his Apostolic Exhortation, *The Joy of the Gospel* (49), Pope Francis teaches that Christian life must be a lived experience helping us to proclaim the Gospel.[27] He insists that we need a supportive community of faith if we are to be true disciples of Christ: "If something should rightly disturb us and trouble our consciences, it is the fact that so many of our brothers and sisters are living without the strength, light and consolation born of friendship with Jesus Christ, without a community of faith to support them." (Ibid). Forming communities of faith is a key challenge for mission in the present secular era—as we argue in Chapter Eight.

Third World churches often live Gospel values more authentically than does the West. Reverse mission[28] refers to the fact that missionaries from former mission fields are now ministering in the West in areas in need of clergy. In fact, this is part of the Church's overall internal mission today. The Church also has an external mission including its outreach to non-Christian religions. This outreach is in addition and parallel to its missionary endeavors to bring the Gospel to the non-baptized.[29] we shall later explore some long-term implications of an outreach to non-Christian religions. We shall also study the latter aspect of the Church's external mission as its interfaith outreach—as a sacred conversation among believers. It is sacred because it knows that undue secularization harms society. Interfaith outreach is a global phenomenon occurring on a rather large scale among scholars and religious leaders across the world.

Jesus' parables in St. Matthew's Gospel on how the seed of faith and love can grow—despite the many daunting dangers—illustrate the various ways a Christian harvest is possible in our age. In Matt 13:24, we read that the kingdom of God is like a man who "sowed good seed in his field." But when he was asleep "an enemy came and sowed weeds among the wheat and went away." In Matthew 13:21, Jesus tells us that the seed sown in our hearts must sink deeply and take root. Seeds sown in good soil refer to those who have understood the message of Jesus, helping them bear much fruit.

Pope Francis is a living example of how we may begin to address the ambiguous roles of the Church's internal-external mission today—if founded on a comprehensive assessment of Christian possibilities. We are called to build bridges that can facilitate needed forms of cooperation among people of good will.

Building Bridges and Addressing the Complex Challenges Facing Humanity Today

Although the human condition today is vastly different from what it was in the Middle Ages, and although the notion of mission has changed along with the times, we shall close this chapter by recalling noteworthy accomplishments of the Middle Ages. We shall briefly comment on St. Benedict of Nursia, on the roles of the Monte Cassino monastery, Pope St. Gregory the Great, St. Hildegard of Bingen, Germany, and on Islam's influence in Europe. This will lay a background against which we shall explore the contexts and the trying challenges facing Pope Francis in our own fast-paced, but often superficial, transitional age.

Saint Benedict's Rule of Stability: The Tradition His Monte Cassino Bequeathed the Church

The "Dark Ages" followed the fall of the Roman Empire due to the invasion of tribes from the East such as the Vandals, Ostrogoths and Visigoths. In these dark times, St. Benedict's rule helped save Western civilization. St Benedict (480-547) founded Monte Cassino in 529, some 130 kilometers southeast of Rome—making him the founder of Western monasticism. He realized that the Empire had been weakened by corruption, but as a Roman, he had a flair for organization, "a concern for order, a respect for authority. Monastic life for him was to be structured; it was to follow a rule and a hierarchical chain of command."[30] The monastic tradition that he began helped convert pagan tribes during the early Middle Ages. It led to his being one of the patron saints of Europe. His Rule became the central focus of cenobitic monasticism and other forms of communal-spiritual life. The core of the Rule prescribes a daily rhythm of prayer and labor (*Ora et Labora*) within the context of a monastic Institution. Benedictine monasteries are to be directed by a strong, responsible central leadership. While the Abbot or Abbess "holds the place of Christ," he/she, being always accountable to God and to the Rule, must recognize that in a corrupt world that he/she is part of a higher chain of command.[31] Because of the threat of barbarian invasions, Benedict wanted his monasteries enclosed: all the necessities of life should be found within. "There should be no need for monks to roam outside because this is not at all good for their souls" (Ibid, Ch 66). Leaving the monastery was spiritually unsafe. Journeys needed the abbot's permission; travelers "should not presume to relate to anyone what they saw or heard outside the monastery, because this causes the greatest harm" (Ibid, Ch 67). Benedict was a man of his time but his rule was adaptable. He was not primarily concerned with the external ordering of monks' lives but rather with their genuine quest for the divine. As was the case with the older desert spirituality, he rejected a dichotomy between one's inner self and outer self: the way one lives is the way one prays (and vice-versa). The best expression of an authentic relation to God is the way one relates to one's neighbor.

Monte Cassino, sacked by the Lombards in 570, was rebuilt around 718. It was sacked again in the 9th century by invading Saracens, but rebuilt a third time in 949. The period between the 11th and 12th centuries was the abbey's golden age as it flourished as the center for the Cluniac reforms and engaged in extensive cultural and spiritual dialogue with the Constantinople-led Eastern Orthodox churches.

Around 1050, Constantine the African, a physician and a scholar of medical philosophy, came to Monte Cassino, bringing with him many important manuscripts he had collected from his travels in North Africa which was then subject to Baghdad's Abbasid Caliphate (750-1258). The core of these manuscripts was the writings of Galen (130-210), a Greek physician, surgeon and philosopher in the Roman Empire. There were also interpretations of Galen's works by many Muslim and Christian scholars. Several Monte Cassino monks worked with Constantine for the next two decades in translating key philosophical and medical manuscripts from Arabic into Latin, many of which were unknown in Europe. The translations helped give birth to European scholasticism and to dialogues on the roles of faith and reason over the next two centuries—including the development of the first medical curriculum, entitled the *Articella*.[32] The *Articella*, which included some writings by Hippocrates of Cos, was long used in Europe both as a textbook and as a reference manual up until the 16th century.

Pope St. Gregory the Great

We alluded to the ambiguous role of the Church's mission in the age of colonialism. This ambiguous role had begun with Pope St. Gregory the Great (reigned 590-604), the first pope to call himself "servant of God's servants." Gregory had the political-religious genius to help evangelize various warring entities such as the Lombards in Italy and the Irish. His is a complex legacy; his sense of mission was not always consistent with the ideal of peaceful conversion. He "sometimes advocated a war of aggression against heathens"[33] so as to convert them. His vision of faith and mission was inspired by St. Augustine's *The City of God*, as well as by St. Benedict's teachings. He promoted the use of Gregorian chant in the liturgy. The Benedictine monks who had moved to Rome after the first destruction of Monte Cassino (around 570) influenced both his thought and actions.

St. Hildegard of Bingen (1097-1179) and the Growing Influence of Islam in the 12th Century

St. Hildegard, known as the Sibyl of the Rhine was a German Benedictine abbess, writer, composer, philosopher, Christian mystic, visionary, and polymath. She is considered to be the foundress of scientific natural history in Germany. In Pope Francis' apostolic exhortation *Gaudete et Exsultate* (*Rejoice and Be Glad*), that enjoins us to embark on our Christian journey of holiness, Hildegard is one of the 40 saints he holds up for her achievements while embracing the ordinariness of everyday life. Her many writings can still teach us how to rejoice and be glad in all of life's challenges, mysteries, and joys today. She lived in the 12th century which was marked by a turning point in the influence of the papacy in Europe and of Islamic scholarship. She was able to account for the positive and negative aspects in Islam through her use of symbolism.[34]

The Church of the East had broken away from Rome in 1054. In 1077, the papacy asserted its primacy over the Holy Roman Emperor Henry IV.[35] In 1095, Pope Urban II helped organize the First Crusades to retake Jerusalem after its capture by Seljuk Turks (1071). The infusion of new knowledge into the West from North Africa and the Middle East continued over the next two centuries culminating in Aquinas' synthesis of Faith and Reason in the 13th Century. Muslim thinkers such as Avicenna (Ibn Sina) and Averroes (Ibn Rushd) played key roles in these developments. The ambiguous nature of this relationship was evident in that the Crusades were a cross current to the philosophical, scientific, and theological dialogues occurring in medieval universities. The Mongolian invasion in the 13th century led to the decline in Islamic scholarship and to a rise of Islamic fundamentalism focused on law—not on reason.

Toward Filling the Spiritual Vacuum Haunting Humanity Today

St. Benedict, St. Gregory the Great, the monks of Mount Cassino, and St. Hildegard all pointed beyond themselves by dedicating their lives to God and to the Gospel's Good News. Likewise, we today have to rethink ways we might fill the spiritual vacuum threatening the foundations of Christian life in an age dominated by technology and secularism. As did Aquinas and others in the Middle Ages, we today have to build bridges rather than walls. Pope Francis has shown the way; we invite the reader to join him in this task.

The fact that the pope took the name of Francis, a profligate who became a humble friar in an age of transition, suggests that he has profound insights into what it means to follow St. Francis' example in the 21st century. While the pope's critics would have him stick to tradition more closely so as to ensure stability in today's Church, for Pope Francis, a modern prophet and pathbreaker, tradition means adhering more closely to Gospel priorities. Christians must be the salt of the earth (Matthew 5:13-16). The pope wants to renew the Church in the Spirit of Vatican II and beyond. For him, the Church is to be the harbinger of Jesus' Good News lest it lose its ability to help transform an endangered, ever-changing world. If the salt of the earth loses its saltiness, it risks being no longer good for anything—except "to be trampled underfoot,"[36] as atheist secularists are attempting to do. Francis wants to help us know Jesus better, to help all humans live in peace. His is an ethically-oriented papacy that harks back to St. Augustine's refusal to separate theology from ethics. He advocates being glocally hospitable towards all in spite of all our divides. The following chapters explore ways Francis and others have reassessed the Church's historically transformative mission[37] in a vastly transformed, all-too divided world.

Notes

1. The Ghanian Cardinal Peter Turkson has played a key role in writing and promoting *Laudato Si*.
2. Despite the political and economic realities of late 19th century Russia, Tolstoy published his "The Kingdom is within you." It was promptly banned in Russia. Gandhi read it and was transformed by it. In turn, Gandhi's non- violent resistance led to India's independence and, eventually, to ML King Jr's liberation movement in the USA.
3. David Gray, "The Homiletic Christology of Pope Francis Regarding the Ongoing Mission of Christ Jesus" at www.davidlgray.info/2015/05/28/christology-pope-francis/. See also David J. Hawkin, "Albert Schweitzer and the Interpretation of the New Testament" https://churchsociety.org/docs/churchman/125/Cman_125_4_Hawkin.pdf
4. Vatican II enabled the Church to "deal with" the period of quasi-chaos unleashed in 1968 during Paul VI's papacy.
5. Many such bridge-building strategies are explored in John Raymaker, *Bernard Lonergan's Third Way of the Heart and Mind: Bridging some Buddhist-Christian-Muslim Secularist Misunderstandings with a Global Secularity Ethics* (Lanham MD. Hamilton Books, 2016).
6. Constantine's attempt to create a Christian empire resulted in the state

taking over much of the responsibilities of the church such as caring for the poor. Constantine is credited with saying that a change in religion implies a changed social order. His policies embraced two parallel but distinct objects: to create a world fit for Christians to live in and to make the world safe for Christianity. The former found expression in broad moral and social reforms. The latter viewed the Church as an institution conceived somewhat along the lines of pagan state-cults. See C. N. Cochrane, *Christianity and classical culture: A study of thought and action from Augustus to Augustine*, Oxford Univ. Press, New York, 1974, 191-211. Constantine also sought to rebuild the bridges between a Christianity divided by the controversy of Arianism (a heresy that held that Christ was not divine—he, too, was a created being). That first Nicaea Council formulated the key doctrinal formula of the Church still expressed in the Nicene Creed.

7   Christ did not appoint Peter to be the *Pontifex Maximus*; he gave him the keys to the Kingdom (Matthew 16:19). The early Church Fathers spoke of the *Pontifex Maximus* in derogatory terms for it designated the reigning Emperor as head of a pagan religion. "*Pontifex Maximus*" was an imperial office which made him the "chief priest."

8   See M. Farouk Radwan, "How to bridge the gap between the conscious and the unconscious mind," www.2knowmyself.com/why_the_subconscious_doesnt_use_logic; Carolyn Gregoire, "Creative people's brains really do work differently." https://qz.com/584850/creative-peoples-brains-really-do-work-differently/

9   Women had a major role in evangelizing the Roman Empire. In the first two centuries of the Church, women hosted Christian gatherings and worship before Tertullian and others began to object to this practice. See Elaine Pagels, "Women in the Early Church," www.pbs.org/wgbh/pages/frontline/shows/religion/first/roles.html

10 On bishop accountability as to this issue: www.bishop-accountability.org/ www.bbc.com/news/uk-21649475

11 For Jürgen Moltmann, *The Church in the Power of the Spirit: A Contribution to Messianic Ecclesiology* (Fortress, 1993), the Church is sent in mission because God is "a sending God. Not only did God the Father send the Son in the power of the Spirit into the world, but the Trinity has an inherently "sending" nature within Godself" The mutual expression of love within the Trinity is "the foundation for God's expression of love to the world," as well as "the foundation for the Church's expression of God's love for the world in mission." (54).

12 Stephen Bevans, "On Prophetic Dialogue and Joy of the Gospel" http://learn.ctu.edu/content/joy-gospel-steve-bevans-svd-0. We examine the causes of modern anxieties and actual dysfunctional situations of many kinds.
13 Bevans and Schroeder, *Constants in Context*, 6. For them, the goal of mission is not to expand the Church for its own sake. Rather, people are invited into the Church so that they can join a community serving God's reign. God's mission has both *ad-intra* and *ad-extra* dimensions. We praise the authors' efforts but we signal their limitations as does Lode Wostyn's review. (*East Asian Pastoral Review*, 2007, 44 2007, 1). Wostyn notes that while *Constants* is rich in content, it is *very* complex as it summarizes "an enormous amount of material." It "is a goldmine but it tends to lead to confusion." Some missiologist-reviewers "did not recognize the paradigm the authors" ascribe to them. We address today's complexities through the glocal insights pioneered by such seminal thinkers as Teilhard de Chardin, Bernard Lonergan and by proponents of glocal spiritualities, glocal philosophies and glocal ethics.
14 Bevans and Schroeder, *Prophetic Dialogue*, 64-71. For Richard Rohr, "Christ in Paul's Eyes," https://cac.org/christ-in-pauls-eyes-weekly-summary-2019-03-02/9, St. Paul summarizes his corporate understanding of salvation with his shorthand phrase "in Christ" which seems to be Paul's code phrase for the gracious, participatory experience of salvation "from the beginning" (Ephesians 1:3-12). Identity with Christ "means humanity has never been separated from God—unless and except by its own negative choice. All of us, without exception, are living inside of a cosmic identity, already in place, that is drawing and guiding us forward."
15 John Paul II, *Redemptoris Missio* (Washington, D.C.: United States Catholic Conference, 1991), 41. The document uses "mission" and "evangelization" interchangeably in a broad multifaceted way.
16 In many ways, a secularized West needs rebaptizing. One cannot rebaptize a society, but a secularized West needs enlightenment of some sort. Pope Francis' embrace of mercy suggests ways of mutual enlightenment.
17 For Brett Scott, https://roarmag.org/essays/the-gentrification-of-payments/ (Feb., 2019), the merging of finance and technology fosters corporate control at the expense of informality and excludes the most marginalized. Paul Mason www.socialeurope.eu/the-new-spirit-of-postcapitalism writes: "During the past 20 years, as a survival

mechanism, the market has reacted by creating semi-permanent distortions. ... In response to the price-collapsing effect of information goods, the most powerful monopolies ever seen have been constructed. Seven out of the top ten global corporations by market capitalization are tech monopolies; they stifle competition through the practice of buying rivals and build 'walled gardens' of interoperable technologies to maximize their own revenues at the expense of suppliers and customers. They avoid paying taxes avoidance. Because information machines can replace humans faster than they create new, skilled jobs, millions of low-paid jobs have been created. The blurring of work and leisure time has been encouraged; consumption activities (booking a holiday, arranging a date, messaging friends) has been tolerated within work time, because this maximizes consumption and personal-data production.

18 In the background, lurk the tribal realities that have led to endless conflicts in many parts of the world.

19 www.laityfamilylife.va/content/dam/laityfamilylife/Pdf/Pope%20Francis'%20Revolution%20of%20Mercy.pdf

20 The bus boycott was just one example of many situations where, under ML King Jr's influence, the civil rights movement gained attention and respect. A key part of King's vision, aside from a quest for racial equality, was Gandhi's idea of non-violence. King refused to use violent actions in any of his protests; he taught his followers to do the same. This factor greatly influenced society in the late 1960's. Use of force by police lost its effectiveness.

21 Reus-Smit, https://foreignpolicy.com/2019/03/21/international-relations-theory-doesnt-understand-culture

22 Bernard Lonergan argues for a *critical* realism that recognizes the weaknesses of both naive realism and idealism. His book *Insight*, (*CWL 3, Collected Works*, Univ. of Toronto Press) clarifies the roles of understanding and judging.

23 Hannah Arendt, *The Origins of Totalitarianism* (Orlando, FL: Harcourt, 1968), 209, rejects Rudyard Kipling's fantasies about the British Empire, noting that "legendary explanations of history always served as belated corrections" of the facts and deeds man "had not done and for consequences man had not foreseen."

24 Jorge Romero, "Don Quixote Rides Again: Illusion and Delusion in Conrad's *Lord Jim*." His desire to become a sailor and the renowned knight of La Mancha seems deliberate. www.clas.ufl.edu/ipsa/2005/proc/romero.pdf

25 The quandary of truth: "Ah yes, truth. Funny how everyone is always asking for it but when they get it they don't believe it because it's not the truth they want to hear." Helena Cassadine, actress in "General Hospital."
26 On May 1, 2019 Pope Francis in his book, *Rebuking the Devil* (USCCB) reminds us that Satan is real, that we should learn how to rebuke the devil's wiles.
27 Issued in 2013, *The Joy of the Gospel* is the document Francis calls the most important of his pontificate.
28 Reverse mission has its roots in a clergy-laity issue addressed in the reforms of Pope Gregory VII (1073-1085) that imposed clerical celibacy. Gregory VII also created the College of Cardinals to insulate the selection of future popes from lay interference. Gregory's actions were the culmination of the Reform Movement initiated by Pope Leo IX (1049-1054). See Valérie Theis, https://international.la-croix.com/news/role-of-lay-people-was- already-an-issue-during-the-11th-century/8905 and Diarmad MacCulloch, *A History of Christianity: The First Three Thousand Years* (Viking, 2009). Gregory's reforms indirectly led to today's dilemma of a lack of clergy, providing the opportunity for the rise of small Christian communities across the world. Reverse mission exemplifies the interaction between the Church's internal and external mission at their very core. The issues of lay-clergy relations and of reverse mission are interrelated in tension-laden ways. In Chapter 8, we argue that small Christian communities can help energize Christians to live their faith in authentic, personalized ways as was the case with early Christians. This, in turn would be of help to the Church's overall mission in a pluralistic world.
29 We are here rephrasing Bevans and Schroeder's distinction between mission as proclamation which seeks to convert persons to Christianity and mission as dialogue which engages in sacred dialogues with other religions.
30 Laurence Freeman, OSB, "Some Reflections on the Rule of St Benedict: Four Principles or Attitudes, *Via Vitae* January 2006. "The shape and the form of the life can be changed according to circumstance (Ch 40). It is pragmatic rather than programmatic. . . .. Life in common was for Benedict the crucible of the spiritual life, both its testing ground and the place where a "zeal for God" expresses itself in patience, mutual obedience and respect (Ch 72)." The four principles or attitudes are Obedience, Peace, Faith and Works together and Humility. Benedict

wanted to give a practical framework on which the higher edifices of the spiritual life could be built.

31 Chapter 2 of the Rule. See http://wccm.org/content/%E2%80%9Csome-reflections-rule-st-benedict-four-principles-or-attitudes%E2%80%9D-laurence-freeman-osb

32 This period also witnessed the establishment of Islamic intellectual centers in North Africa from Cairo to Tunisia. Major Western universities such as Oxford, Cambridge, and Paris depended on Arabic science, mathematics and philosophy. On the roles of Monte Cassino and Constantine, see Gerald Grudzen, *Medical Theory About the Body and Soul in the Middle Ages: The First Western Medical Curriculum at Monte Cassino*, Mellen Press, 2007; also Grudzen-Rahman, *Spirituality and Science: Greek, Judeo-Christian and Islamic Perspectives* (Author House, 2007).

33 "Gregory I" in *The New Encyclopedia Britannica*," Vol. 5, 477. (Chicago, 1986, 477). Gregory I sent 40 monks from his own monastery with St. Augustine (later of Canterbury) to evangelize Britain. He wrote a biography of Benedict.

34 *The Five Beasts*, https://thefivebeasts.wordpress.com/2015/01/14/the-era-of-the-grey-wolf-and-islam/

35 From 750 to 1000, the Church had to free itself from control by monarchs while also facing the advance of Islam.

36 A week before his election as pope, Francis pointed to the internal sickness that had invaded the Church, that of a "self-referential" hierarchic structure that, in fact, was keeping the Church from authentically preaching Jesus' message today. The draft of his *Praedicate Evangelium* which would fundamentally reshape the Roman Curia into an instrument serving local bishops is one step the pope has taken to change a deeply flawed hierarchical culture. See *National Catholic Reporter*, June 14-27, 3, 20 and June 28-July 11, 11, "Proposed document reorders Vatican offices." The draft of *Praedicate* contains a brief description that shares 12 guiding principles of the curial reform. The second principle repeats Francis' frequent call for a "sound decentralization of authority in the Church."

37 The eminent missiologist David Bosch, *Transforming Mission: Paradigm Shifts in Theology of Mission*, (Orbis, 1991), 180, argues that . . . humanization has been a part of the Christian mission from the beginning. "In a society described as 'macabre, lost in despair, perversion, and superstition,' Christian communities emerged as something entirely new." On the periphery of society, they were mostly composed of slaves, women and foreigners.

CHAPTER 2

How Pope Francis Has Given New Foci to the Church's Mission

History in general is complex and so is the history of the Church. We approach such complexities by expanding on Bevans and Schroeder's notion of mission as prophetic dialogue. For them, "God is Mission. This is what God is in God's deepest self: self-diffusive love, freely creating, redeeming, healing challenging that creation."[1] Pope Francis has testified to God's diffusive love throughout his life. For him, "Jesus is the gift of God for us. If we welcome Him, we too can be a gift."[2] Believing in welcoming God through our neighbor, we engage in a form of prophetic dialogue in a digitalized, globalized world. Relying, in part, on outstanding Christian thinkers such as Teilhard de Chardin, Bernard Lonergan and Paul Ricoeur, we seek to show how reason and faith can be based on adapted forms of glocal ethics,[3] glocal spiritualities, glocal theologies. Traditionally, there have been two types of Catholic theology—positive and negative.[4] The first seeks to establish the truth of the Church's teaching on the basis of Scripture and Tradition. Negative theology stresses that one cannot "explain" what God is. God is mystery. Unfortunately, the two types tend to ignore, even exclude the other. The artificial boundary between the two is in fact much more porous.[5] This chapter first identifies various types of atheism that have dogged the West since the Enlightenment. Following comments on the Church's "colonial sins," it recalls the lives of two saints the pope canonized: Mother Teresa who served the poor, and Archbishop Romero. Both saints can help us understand why and how the pope has initiated a glocally evolution of mercy[6] based on the Gospels as exemplified in his two exhortations on the joy of the gospels and of love.

Atheist Claims That Have Dogged Humanity and the Church since the Enlightenment

Since the claims of the French Enlightenment and those of the "Masters of Suspicion" (Marx, Nietzsche and Freud) in the 19th century, atheists have questioned and opposed religious beliefs. Books such as Sam Harris' *The End of Faith* (2004), Richard Dawkins's *The God Delusion* (2006), Daniel

Dennet's *Breaking the Spell: Religion as a Natural Phenomenon* (2006) and Christopher Hitchens' *God is not Great* (2007) became best sellers.[7] Hitchens alleges that "holy war" is the greatest existential threat to civilization, but he has nothing to say about "the cold war, which brought us close to the brink of planetary Armageddon,"[8] or about North Korea's communist "quasi-theocracy". Dennett's *Breaking* argues that religion is in need of scientific analysis so that its nature and future may be better understood, but he does extend a conciliatory hand to believers so long as they are willing to subject any purportedly God-given moral edict "to the full light of reason, using all the evidence at our command."[9]

Paul Ricoeur and Pope Francis on Atheists' Claims: Addressing the Roots of Alienation

For Paul Ricoeur, Western atheists have misconstrued the meaning of the Biblical metaphor of God as Father: the Father as moral lawgiver should not be viewed, as some atheists do, as though God is intent on reprisal and punishment. Rather, God encourages us to be creative. Ricoeur adds that atheism "is at once a canyon dividing religion from faith and also a bridge that can allow us to traverse the gap, from an inauthentic expression of faith to an authentic articulation of something more, a 'post-religious' faith."[10] Ricoeur argues that atheists paradoxically open ways "to a faith situated not beyond good and evil" a la Nietzsche, "but to a view that God is love not law."[11] Faith hopes—it is not morality. Pope Francis once told young boy, anxious about his deceased father's atheism, that his father could find his way to heaven.[12] Francis' appeals to God's goodness speak to our hearts. Mystics' insights, which are at the base of negative theology, can offset the hardness of calculating minds. Recall how the great mystic Catherine of Siena (1347-80) helped reform the Church during the 14th century's crises. In 1378, she persuaded Pope Gregory XI to leave Avignon and return to Rome. As in the case of St. Hildegard before her, she translated her visions into effective action that has affected history.

However much faithful Catholics pine for the good old days when faith and reason were "in sync," secularism means that the young are now less aware of their moral-spiritual potential. Secularists and believers are alienated from one another because the former are cut off from religious traditions. Secularism implies human self-sufficiency; still, it cannot avoid confrontations. In Europe, for example, young Muslim immigrants often feel marginalized in the frantic world of money and power. They resent being ostracized. Some resort to violence.[13] Today's alienation has roots in ideological predations.[14] We live in an alienated global or glocal village. With the pope, we seek ways to remedy alienation's causes.

Pope Francis' Apology for the Church's "Ideological Colonization," and Why He Advocates Synods

Pope Francis apologized for the Church's "grave colonial sins" in a speech (July 9, 2015) at the World Meeting of Popular Movements in Bolivia.[15] He has used the term "ideological colonization" to describe what he sees as affluent societies oppressing developing ones—as trying to impose alien sets of "values" on them. The adoption of said "values" is a condition of their receiving humanitarian or developmental aid. For Francis, ideological colonization tolerates no cultural or spiritual differences. In some cases, it has even resorted to "persecuting those who believe in God."[16] This is a blasphemy against God.

As Archbishop of Buenos Aires, Bergoglio, concerned with poverty and the environment, promoted Catholic Social Teaching along the lines of Pope Leo XIII's 1891 Encyclical *Rerum Novarum* (On the Rights and Duties of Capital and Labor) which condemned the Industrial Revolution's evils. He concentrated on the relationships between people and profit, labor and capital, politics and economics—concluding that the "common good" and solidarity with workers are essential. Upon becoming pope, Francis began to focus on subsidiarity. In politics, subsidiarity means that issues should be decided whenever possible on the local level rather than by central governments. Francis began to apply subsidiarity in governing the Church by relying more on Church synods—advisory councils on various levels of administration made up of bishops and a few lay people.[17] We interpret subsidiarity glocally. By relying on synods, Pope Francis wants local churches to have more "say" in their own affairs.[18] It is an open question as to how synods can foster co-responsibility in governing the Church. Yes, all are responsible in the Church, but not in the same way. Pope Paul VI convoked the First Synod of Bishops in 1967. The Synod held in October, 2018 on the theme, "Young People, Faith and Vocational Development,"[19] focused on helping young people discern what is best in life. The pope is faced with a delicate balancing act. His push for different ways of being Church shows his intention "to hold together opposing currents — maintaining an institutional structure in a Catholic culture that tends more and more to become not just post-clerical, but also post-ecclesial and post-Church."[20]

We need to reevaluate how the People of God as a whole can help discern the roles of bishops and of the laity in ways adopted by Vatican II. Such reevaluation is foreshadowed in the messages Pope Francis delivered upon canonizing Mother Teresa and Archbishop Romero.

Pope Francis Canonizes Mother Teresa and Archbishop Romero

When he canonized Mother Teresa[21] in 2016, Pope Francis shamed world leaders to the extent they are guilty of the "crime of poverty."[22] He had had 1,500 homeless people from various parts of Italy bused to St. Peters Square to take seats of honor at the ceremony. The pope held up Mother Teresa as a tireless worker of mercy—a model of holiness for all in an age of self-promotion, a woman who preached more by example than words. She avoided the trap of bending to a "public faith" which, in fact, is largely faithless. Her selflessness testified to God's mercy. "She showed that God's mercy is alive and thriving in our world."[23] Her Missionaries of Charity are to befriend "the poorest people, especially those most rejected and abandoned by others, lepers, the dying, the hungry, the ones sick with AIDS: they are all Jesus…. Jesus cannot deceive us when he assures us: 'I was sick and you took care of me'"[24] In 2018, when he canonized Archbishop Romero, the pope spoke of the Gospel as it should be lived. We cannot explain what God is, but we can speak of his mercy, of his unbounded love in an age of egoistic self-seeking. Both of the new saints lived lives of "self-emptying" (*kenosis*)[25] reflecting the life of Christ who emptied himself. Romero was influenced by liberation theology which sees the mission of the church as not only saving souls for Christ, but also dismantling oppressive and exploitative power structures. Francis noted that his own theology is akin to Romero's. Wearing the bloodstained rope belt Romero wore when assassinated, he stressed the "radical" nature of Jesus Christ. "Jesus gives all and he asks all: he gives a love that is total and asks for an undivided heart."[26] Francis quoted Romero's words that "to think with the Church means to take part in the Church's glory, which is to live, heart and soul, the *kenosis* of Christ. In the Church, Christ lives among us; she must therefore be humble and poor, since an aloof, prideful and self-sufficient Church is not the Church of *kenosis*."[27] Self-emptying is not a thing of the past, but a present pledge that we can sense." We can discover Jesus' presence at work in history—a presence that we neither can nor want to silence, since we know from experience that he alone is "the Way, the Truth and the Life. Christ's *kenosis* reminds us that God saves in history, in the life of each person, and that this is also his own history, from which he comes forth to meet us." (Ibid). Denouncing wealth inequality, the pope asked for "the grace always to leave things behind for love of the Lord." He added that "to leave behind wealth, the yearning for status and power, structures that are no longer adequate for proclaiming the Gospel, those weights that slow down our mission, the strings that tie us to the world." (Ibid). Like Romero, Pope Francis has led a life of noble detachment. He has asked Christians to frequently examine their conscience. His is a glocally ethical "revolution" promoting mercy.

Pope Francis and Cardinal Walter Kasper on Being Merciful

Pope Francis has entrusted his papacy to God's mercy. For the atheist Hitchens, "life is a wager." His wager amounts to a know-it-all, cold-hearted, merciless self-promotion. For Pope Francis, God is Mercy. His proclamation of a Holy Year of Forgiveness and Mercy (Dec., 2015-Nov., 2016) had its roots in a discussion he had some years before. He recalls that "mercy" is derived from *misericordia* (opening one's heart to wretchedness). "Mercy is the divine attitude which embraces. It is God's giving himself to us, accepting us, ready to forgive," as illustrated in the Parable of the Prodigal Son (Luke 15:11-32). The pope's stress on mercy has also been influenced by Cardinal Kasper's book *Mercy: The Essence of the Gospel and the Key to Christian Life* (2014). Kasper had given a copy of his book to Bergoglio during the conclave that elected him to the papacy. Inspired by Kasper's continuous calls for reform, Pope Francis has tackled the difficult task of finding ways to allow divorced and remarried Catholics to receive Communion. Because Francis and Kasper both insist on an evangelical mercy, the two have worked to provide the needed theological underpinnings for renewing Catholicism.

Francis has had to address the sexual abuse problem he inherited. He has invoked discipline, calling for repentance. Nothing is entirely black or white. The retired Pope Benedict XI blamed clerical sexual abuse on the sexual revolution. Pope Francis, like the rest of humanity has to deal with a "confused" world. How fathom God's will amidst confusion? The Church is one, holy, catholic and apostolic—but always in need of reform. All too many Catholics abandon ship, rather than help reform the Church. We seek to build bridges of mercy amidst many uncertainties—wishing that people would truly live by the virtues of faith, hope, and charity. Francis has been a charismatic, "radical" pope reaching out with joy to all. His legacy cannot be separated from the demands of conservative Catholics who insist on living by the strict teachings of Pope John Paul II and Benedict XVI. We must distinguish being liberal from being "radical." The latter goes to the root of a problem. In that sense the pope is radical, not liberal. He goes back to the gospels' radical roots of conversion, rather than being too liberal in ways that would do away with discipline. This is important, even crucial to any evaluation of Pope Francis' teachings. It is crucial because the pope calls us to live holy lives. Chapter Three of his *Gaudete et Exultate*, for example is titled "In the Light of the Master." Sec. 67-99 urge us to "go against the flow" by trying to live the Beatitudes:

> "Blessed are the poor in spirit, for theirs is the kingdom of heaven" [67-70]
> "Blessed are the meek, for they will inherit the earth" [71-74]
> "Blessed are those who mourn, for they will be comforted" [75-76]
> "Blessed are those who hunger and thirst for righteousness, for they will be filled" [77-79]
> "Blessed are the merciful, for they will receive mercy" [80-82]
> "Blessed are the pure in heart, for they will see God" [83-86]
> "Blessed are the peacemakers, for they will be called children of God" [87-89]
> "Blessed are those who are persecuted for righteousness' sake, for theirs is the kingdom of heaven."

The "great criterion" for living the Beatitudes [95] is being faithful to the Master [96-99]. *Gaudete et Exultate* then goes into some of the "ideologies that strike at the heart of the Gospel" [100-103].

The Church's Glocal Bridge-Building Tradition: from St. Paul to Pope Francis

The Church's bridge-building tradition was initiated by Jesus. The 11 apostles and the convert St. Paul helped bridge the Hebrew, Greek, and Roman worlds. Later, the Church civilized the tribes that overran Europe. Limits appeared in the Church's bridge-building ability when Europe was confronted with Islam, and later with Western secularism. In the meanwhile, the message of Christ has had to be "inculturated" as missionaries brought the Good News to parts of China, India, and Africa. The book *Steps Toward Vatican III* (2008) examines the dilemmas facing the Church in an age of globalization. People of various backgrounds daily come into close proximity. How may the Church help bridge our differences with an ethical spirituality operative at various levels of Church structures? *Steps* suggests paths that may help bring peace and understanding in the world by sympathetically evaluating different world traditions. It anticipates themes Pope Francis has adopted as he goes about building bridges. A helpful way to build bridges between various spiritual traditions is practiced in the inter-spirituality movement initiated by the Catholic monk, Wayne Teasdale (1945-2004). Inter-Spirituality would draw from all major wisdom traditions of the world. Teasdale argued that the world religions all bear witness to the experience of Ultimate Reality variously named Brahman, Allah, (the) Absolute, God, Great Spirit. Inter-spirituality views the world's wisdom traditions as moving beyond interfaith dialogue toward symbiotic concerns for the environment. This symbiotic concern complements the pope's *Laudato Si* as well as the aims of evolutionary spirituality which urges us to protect Mother Earth. This, too, is relevant to the Church's mission in the 21st century. Traditional Catholics who oppose Francis' efforts fail to understand that he is more traditionalist than his critics. He insists that we have to wed the new with the old if we are to bear fruit today. Luke 6: 43-45 says that a tree is known by its fruits. To bear fruit, we must realize that the world is not static, but dynamic. Faithful to the Gospel, the pope is leading the Church beyond his critics' myopic views. He hearkens back to Jesus' parables on the Kingdom taught in St. Matthew's gospel:

> Matt 13: 44-45: "The kingdom of heaven is like a treasure hidden in a field. When a man found it, he hid it again, and then in his joy went and sold all he had and bought that field. Again, the kingdom of heaven is like a merchant looking for fine pearls." Having found one pearl of great price, he went and sold all that he had, and bought it. The parable of the precious pearl helps us express our deepest expectations and even to break through the thick layer of our emotions such as joy, anger, hate, and sentiments.

> In Matt 13:41, Jesus speaks of the Son of Man sending out his angels to "gather up out of his kingdom all those who cause people to sin and all others who do evil things." Christians must share their lives with those who are not yet of the kingdom. Jesus uses the image of the kingdom to stress that which humans cannot achieve without God. He asks his disciples whether they have understood his teaching in the hope that they will truly fathom the meaning of his passion and death. A Christian should not give in to temptations. With Ricoeur, we hold that Jesus' parables of

the kingdom apply on two levels: interpreting them before committing one's self to the kingdom of God. The Gospels' teaching on the kingdom should inspire believers to live so that they will be transformed on both personal and community levels. In Mark 12:34, Jesus tells a scribe, who had admitted that God's commandment of love is more important than offering sacrifices, that he is "not far from the kingdom of God." Jesus sought to gather God's people so that they might love God, community, and neighbor from the heart. Pope Francis echoed this in his World Mission Day, 2018, message. He reminded Catholics that "Every man and woman is a mission; that is the reason for our life on this earth. To be attracted and to be sent are two movements that our hearts, especially when we are young, feel as interior forces of love; they hold out promise for our future and they give direction to our lives. . . .. To live out joyfully our responsibility for the world is a great challenge." He added: "I am a mission on this Earth; that is the reason why I am here in this world."

Concluding Chapter 2 by Way of Recapitulating our Journey

We have considered the realities of atheism and religious indifferentism today. In the Western world, these realities are very likely due to many Christians not having lived the Gospel as they should. Still, throughout history, there have been outstanding saints who have lived Jesus' Good News. Our Pope-Francis-inspired journey is one of glocal solidarity with Jesus. We urge Christians to live Jesus' Good News in authentic ways. Our proposal, rooted in history and directed toward a peaceful future based on mutual tolerance, invites the reader to contrast the priorities of Jesus' message with those of the world. Christian priorities are summarized in such gospel ideals as "Seek and you shall find" (Matt 7:7); "losing one's self so as to find one's self" (Matt 10:39). Time and meaning do affect human communities. Still, one can learn from communities which no longer exist. If time and meaning can refer to the past, the present, and the future, so can a community—given the fact that meaning constitutes community.[28]

Notes

1 Bevans-Schroeder, *Prophetic Dialogue*, 10.
2 https://twitter.com/pontifex/status/1081165850642653189?lang=en
3 See, e. g. https://reflections.yale.edu/article/money-and-morals-after-crash/glocal-economic-ethic-nows-time

4 Positive theology is equivalent to the kataphatic; negative theology deals with the apophatic. It attempts to approach God by negation. It speaks only in terms of what may not be said about the perfect goodness that is God.
5 Richard Kearney's *Anatheism: Returning to God After God* (Columbia Univ., 2009), builds on the work of Ricoeur. He argues for a third anatheist way: a "sacramental return to the holiness of the everyday." It invokes a "yes" in the wake of "no," which marks the potential return to God after "God." Ana-theos is a creative unknowing. It requires us to break with former sureties; it invites us to forge new meanings from ancient wisdoms such as "re-speaking" of God. Having 'traversed' the dark night of the soul, one emerges on the other side, into a 'second faith, an ethical imperative of loving even in the face of injustice. One encounters religious wonder anew. Situated at the split between theism and atheism, one responds in deeper, freer ways to what we cannot fathom or prove. Anatheism is an inaugural event lying at the heart of every great religion— a wager between hospitality and hostility to the stranger. Kearney shows how a return to God is possible for seekers leading to a birth of a more liberating faith. https://twitter.com/pontifex/status/1081165850642653189?lang=en This is hinted at in the sad sense of loss many secularized French people expressed after the Notre Dame fire.
6 His glocal revolution can be likened to Michel de Montaigne's *Essais* (1580) which attack the pretensions of the aristocrats and intellectuals of his day. Montaigne reminds us of our fundamental humanity. He venerates average people: "In practice, thousands of little women in their villages have lived more gently, more equably than Cicero."
7 Stephen L. Carter, *Culture of Disbelief* (New York: Harper), 1993, argues that religion in the US has been trivialized by American law and politics which belittle religious devotion. Religion is even identified with irrationality. Carter insists that religion's role in a democracy is to provide an independent moral voice between the citizen and state.
8 Steven Poole," *The Four Horsemen review* - whatever happened to 'New Atheism'?" January 29, 2019 See www.theguardian.com/books/2019/jan/31/four-horsemen-review-what-happened-to-new-atheism-dawkins-hitchens
9 Poole, ibid. Pascal's wager is that it is more reasonable to believe in God rather than to blindly opt for atheism.
10 See https://godaftergod.wordpress.com/2012/12/09/the-apophatic-way-

part-2-of-the-anaphatic-way/. The kataphatic and apophatic both point to transcendent reality. For the latter, this reality can be only be intuited for it is beyond words. Grace gives one a limited access to the divine. Centering prayer and Zen can help. In Islam, the kataphatic-apophatic distinction stems from the teaching that Allah can only be known as manifested in His Signs.

11 Stephen J. Costello, *Hermeneutics and the Psychoanalysis of Religion* (Oxford: Peter Lang, 2010) 128. For Ricoeur, metaphorical utterances clarify the assimilation of one thing to another, of us to things that a symbol confuses. Nietzsche's atheism differs from the atheism of empiricists and positivists who "dismiss" the supernatural—alleging that it cannot be proved. It also differs from a "new atheism," born after 9/11, 2001 which challenges belief in God. Staks Rosch,www.huffingtonpost.com/staks-rosch/911-and-the-rise-of-new-a_b_5801652.html argues that before 9/11, many atheists had "live and let live" attitudes toward religion—thinking that religious beliefs were silly, but hurt no one. On 9/11, we saw how dangerous dogmatic beliefs can be—one cannot reason with them. This act of terrorism has motivated some atheists to organize lest dogmatic fanatics do more damage. It woke them from slumber."

12 Pope Francis, May 1, 2018. http://vaticanfiles.org/fr/2018/05/149-atheists-go-heaven-pope-francis-says-yes/

13 In Sweden, for example, now hosting many Muslim immigrants, there reportedly are around 1,500 extremists. See Jane Smith, "Muslim-Christian Relations: Historical and Contemporary Realities." http://oxfordre.com/religion/view/10.1093/acrefore/9780199340378.001.0001/acrefore-9780199340378-e-11

14 John K. Galbraith, *The Predator State: How Conservatives Abandoned the Free Market and Why Liberals Should Too* (Free Press. 2008) argues that public institutions have been subverted to serve private profit. In his *The Shield of Achilles: War, Peace and the Course of History* (Penguin, 2002) Philip Bobbitt argues that the former world of 'nation states' is now a globalized world of 'market states', whose values are shorn of what informed the former dominant faith community; it now increasingly reflects the sole value of maximizing choice as the primary "good."

15 https://foreignpolicy.com/2015/07/10/pope-francis-apologizes-for-churchs-colonial-sins/ His apology reflected John Paul II's in 2000. St. John Paul had donned mourning garments due to the grievous, violent actions of the Inquisition and its sins against Jews, nonbelievers, and

the indigenous people of colonized lands. He asked for pardon "for the use of violence for attitudes of mistrust and hostility toward followers of other religions." (Ibid). Many famous converts to Catholicism such as Jacques Maritain and Thomas Merton converted because it is there that they found updated answers to the problems of mind and heart amidst life's uncertainties.

16 Inés San Martín https://cruxnow.com/vatican/2017/11/21/pope-francis-ideological-colonization-blasphemy-god/
17 "Synod" comes from the Greek word, *synodos*, meaning "walking together": what we name "glocal solidarity."
18 In January, 2019, the French Bishops' Conference invited people to discuss co-responsibility in the Church.
19 In his post-Synod document *Christus Vivit*, the pope praised St. John Paul II for initiating World Youth days.
20 William Grimm, *LaCroix*, Nov. 15, 2018, expressing his "disgust" by the ongoing revelations of Church cover-ups.
21 There are not lacking arm-chair critics such as the atheist Hitchens who accuses Mother Teresa of sub-par treatment https://www.theguardian.com/news/2016/sep/04/mother-teresa-declared-saint-by-pope-francis
22 Mother Teresa's life (1919-1997) exemplifies the Church's global ministry to the poor and disenfranchised of the world. She won the Nobel Peace Prize in 1979. Her religious order has over 4500 members active in 133 countries. In 1946 she experienced a second vocation, a "call within a call." She felt an inner urging to leave her convent so as to work directly with the poor. In 1948 the Vatican allowed her to leave the Sisters of Loretto and to start a new work under the guidance of the Archbishop of Calcutta. To prepare to work with the poor, she took an intensive medical training in Patna, India. Her first venture in Calcutta was to gather unschooled children from the slums and start to teach them. She quickly attracted both financial support and volunteers. In 1950, her group, now called the Missionaries of Charity, received official status as a religious community. Members take the traditional vows of poverty, chastity, and obedience, but add the fourth vow of giving free service to the most poor. in her care centers. See https://www.nybooks.com/articles/1996/12/19/mother-teresa
23 www.beliefnet.com/faiths/catholic/7-insights-from-mother-teresa-on-being-merciful.aspx
24 Mother Teresa: *In my Own Words*. Edited by Jose Luis Gonzales-Balado (New York: Gramercy Books, 1996) 41.

25 In Christian theology, *kenosis* is the 'self-emptying' of Jesus' own will. See *Philippians* 2:7, "Jesus made himself nothing," that is, he emptied himself of his own free will.
26 www.vox.com/2018/10/15/17977944/oscar-romero-new-catholic-saint on Francis' homily of October 14, 2018.
27 Homily of St. Oscar Romero, October 1, 1978. The implication is that the Church is not to be a power-player.
28 Bernard Lonergan, *Method in Theology*, 78-79.

CHAPTER 3

Pierre Teilhard de Chardin (1881-1955) and Pope Francis: Catholic Visionaries

Teilhard's theistic framework on evolutionary processes features the living Christ as an incarnate presence infusing all of history and the whole universe with his radiance and love. In *Laudato Si*, Pope Francis draws upon Teilhard's insights. For both men, religion and science complement one another. Humanity must take measures to ensure a sustainable future for the planet's inhabitants.[1] Teilhard's writings on evolution were initially viewed as suspect by the Church due to the fact that Darwin's theory of evolution was presented as scientific "dogma" irreconcilable with Church teaching. As an advocate of evolution who equivocated on the doctrine of original sin, Teilhard was censured by his Jesuit superiors and sent into exile in China in 1923. By the 1950's, however, Teilhard's theories were being extolled by many theologians including Karl Rahner, Hans Urs von Balthasar, Cardinal Martini and Henri de Lubac who wrote: "We need not concern ourselves with a number of detractors of Teilhard, in whom emotion has blunted intelligence."[2] Teilhard best addresses evolution in *The Phenomenon of Man* (1955) which attempts to reconcile Darwinism and Catholic theology.[3]

By the time of Vatican II (1962-1965), Teilhard's resolution of how to relate Church teaching with the "facts" of Darwinism was widely accepted. Teilhard's understanding of evolution did not end with physical evolution for it considered consciousness as part of the evolutionary process. With the birth of the unique form of human consciousness known as *homo sapiens*, a sense of wonder provided the first glimmer of the religious impulse that must have characterized indigenous peoples' sense of themselves as connected to the whole universe. Teilhard reconnects humans to the universe in a scientific manner that does not overlook the original consciousness of native cultures. Humanity, having undergone a long process of development, is now trying to find its proper place in the universe. The creation story in the *Book of Genesis* complements Greek philosophers' notions of *Logos*. Myths have now been superseded by scientific views of evolution. In past ages, human culture existed largely within tribal societies. It is only recently that cultured civilizations have developed concepts of a nation state. Teilhard was convinced that humanity is now moving beyond the stage of the nation state. He wrote: "The Age of Nations is past. The task before us now, if we would not perish, is to build the earth."[4] Implied in Teilhard's vision is that nation states can no longer adequately cope with environmental problems.

Little did Teilhard know how visionary his words would prove to be. In the 1950's, few had clear ideas about the impact of global warming. Teilhard's prophetic words were very much in evidence at the 2018 Parliament of World Religions meeting in Toronto which featured many panels on the science of climate change and its grave implications: environmental, social, economic, and political. It is one of the principal challenges facing humanity today. Its worst impact will probably be felt by developing countries in the coming decades. Changes in climate are occurring regardless of the boundaries of nation states.[5]

Teilhard's mystical vision[6] of the universe included a unique role for the Christian Eucharist in building the earth. While he was in China and unable to celebrate Mass, he saw the Eucharist as encompassing the whole evolutionary process which he called "Christogenesis," as here summarized in a prayer of his:

> Since once again, Lord ..., I have neither bread, nor wine, nor altar, I will raise myself beyond these symbols, up to the pure majesty of the real itself. I will make the whole world my altar and on it will offer you all the labors and sufferings of the world[.] ... I will place on my paten, O God, the harvest to be won by this renewal of labor. Into my chalice I shall pour all the sap which is to be pressed out this day from the earth's fruits. . ... My chalice and my paten are the depths of a soul laid widely open to all the forces which in a moment will rise up from every corner of the earth and converge upon the Spirit. Grant me . . . the mystic presence of all those whom the light is now awakening to a new day. . ... I recall the whole vast anonymous army of living humanity; those who ... truly believe in the progress of earthly reality and who today will again take up their impassioned pursuit of the light. ... at this dawn of a new day.[7]

Papal and Interfaith Ratifications of Teilhard's Alpha-Omega Insights

Pope John Paul II, recalling Teilhard's "Mass on the World," wrote that the Eucharist is celebrated in order to offer "on the altar of the whole earth the world's work and suffering."[8] The then Cardinal Ratzinger had anticipated John Paul II's praise of Teilhard in his *Principles of Catholic Theology*, writing that Teilhard greatly influenced Vatican II. With daring vision, Teilhard incorporated "the historical movements of Christianity into the great cosmic process of evolution from Alpha to Omega."[9] Vatican II's *Pastoral Constitution on the Church in the Modern World* took its cue from Teilhard's assertion that "Christianity means more progress." This, in turn, "became a stimulus in which the Council Fathers from rich and poor countries alike found a concrete hope." (Ibid). Pope Francis has referred to Teilhard's eschatological vision on the Cosmic Christ as being an integral ecology.[10] Of particular import is Teilhard's "understanding of the human phenomenon as arising from, and deeply connected to the dynamic, unfolding universe." (ibid). Echoing Teilhard's view, Pope Francis wrote: "As part of the universe, called into being by one Father, all of us are linked by unseen bonds and together form a kind of universal family, a sublime communion which fills us with a sacred, affectionate and humble respect. 'God has joined us so closely to the world around us that we can feel the desertification of the soil almost as a physical ailment, and the extinction of a species as a painful disfigurement.'" (*Laudato Si*, 89).

Pope Francis notes that Teilhard stressed humans' role in the long evolutionary journey: "The ultimate destiny of the universe is in the fullness of God, which has already been attained by the risen Christ." (Ibid, 83). The pope asks us to reject "every tyrannical and irresponsible domination of human beings over other creatures. The ultimate purpose of other creatures is not to be found in us. Rather, all creatures are moving forward with us and through us towards a common point of arrival, which is God."[11] For Teilhard, all are drawn to the Cosmic Christ regardless of religious affiliation or nationality. The Cosmic Christ would gather all living creatures—even inert matter, which contains rudimentary "Spirit." These are to be "Christified" at the end of time—at the "Omega Point" of evolution. Against this background, the pope deplores the loss of biodiversity and the fact that the earth's resources are being plundered because of short-sighted approaches to the economy, commerce and production." (32). Caring for ecosystems demands far-sightedness, since no one looking for quick and easy profits is truly interested in the preserving nature. The cost of the damage caused by such a selfish lack of concern is much greater than the potential economic benefits to be obtained. Where certain species are destroyed or seriously harmed, there result incalculable losses. (*Laudato Si*, 36).

Teilhard held that revising our assumptions and attitudes about our relationship to Nature is in need of a new mysticism that would unite us more closely to planet earth. Since Descartes, the western world has lived with a dualistic understanding of the material and spiritual realms which has led to the degradation of many parts of nature. Teilhard's mystical vision unites the material and spiritual realms within an evolutionary, personalist universe that integrates masculine and feminine roles, the human and divine:

> Crimson gleams of Matter, gliding imperceptibly into the gold of spirit, ultimately to become transformed into the incandescence of a Universe that is Person—and through all this there blows, animating it and spreading over it, a fragrant balm, a zephyr of Union . . . . The Diaphany of the Divine at the heart of a glowing universe . . . is what I shall try to communicate.[12]

Teilhard provided metaphysical, scientific and spiritual foundations to better understand religion today. His dynamic, organic vision anticipates Pope Francis' integral ecology that stresses that inequalities in the world must not be ignored. Because many of the world's economic and political leaders lack contact with them, the world's poor are often left out of environmental planning.[13] This, abetted by inadequate analyses that ignore parts of reality, has led to the disintegration of cities. Today, we must realize that ecological and social issues are linked. We must integrate the two in our debates. Justice is at stake to the extent that we fail to hear both the cry of the earth and the cry of the poor. (*Laudato Si*, 49).

Teilhard argued that the world's religions should join forces to help move humanity away from tribalism, ethnocentrism and dogmatism. While in China, he focused on the relationship between Western and Eastern religions which have developed separately. His original approach to this reality was to seek ways to transcend past ethnic and cultural divisions. He developed an interfaith type of ecumenism to help rebuild the earth. He looked for its confirmation in the active and animating elements in different religious traditions. Pope Francis' visionary insights have been influenced by Teilhard—as is our own glocal approach. Teilhard gives us a road map for a sustainable future. We must transcend past conflicts so as to safeguard the future. Pragmatism does not suffice in dealing with climate change.[14] Pope Francis is in full accord with Teilhard's inclusive, harmonious vision for preserving the earth and its inhabitants. Both of these visionary Jesuits inspire us to fully live up to our deepest aspirations for unity with one another and with mother earth. It is as if they shared in the poetic conviction of the Bahai faith's founder that we "are the fruits of one tree. the leaves of one branch, the flowers of one garden."[15]

Ursula King argues that crucial to Teilhard's vision were efforts to develop new religious perceptions animated by emergent, but still unformulated types[16] of mysticism. While she has not applied the term "glocal" to Teilhard, she does speak in that spirit. She refers to "the planetization of humanity" as the startling fact of global interdependence in all areas of human endeavor. Some argue that, in borrowing Vladimir Vernadsky's idea[17] of a noosphere and in adapting it to mean a "thinking membrane covering the planet and unifying human consciousness," Teilhard was, in effect, anticipating glocalization.[18] His Omega point, is the point at which this global consciousness would evolve to fuse with God. This reinforces Teilhard's role as a prophet[19] as he deepened humans' global consciousness—aligning it with God's will. In effect, Teilhard has given us "glocal linkings" to help us live in troubled times. There are sensitive souls whose various experiences in life lead them to live with intense devotion. They have discovered how to connect with God. They realize that despite seeming contradictions it all "hangs together." They are at peace with both divine and human realities in which they are enmeshed—as has been the case with St. Francis and Pope Francis. In whatever continent one lives one can now interact with others in any part of the world. Jesus repeatedly speaks of the leaven—spirituality being an instance of God's hidden work in our lives. To connect this notion of how God might be working in our lives so as to help us cope with e. g. our environmental problems, some have used the term "ecological conversion" which has now entered into the lexicon of Catholic Social Teaching. Coined by Pope John Paul II,[20] the term refers to a "significantly changed relationship to our natural environment."[21] Francis' glocal vision reinforces Pope John Paul II's warning that we must avoid the catastrophe toward which the planet is now heading through sorely needed ecological conversions.

Let us highlight some of the complementary visions of Teilhard, Richard Rohr, Fethullah Gulen and Thomas Merton—all of which complement Pope Francis' vision and can help us direct our affections toward taking measures that might help prevent further catastrophes on our threatened planet.

- The religious breakthrough envisioned by Teilhard decades ago was evident at the World Parliament's meeting in Toronto (Nov., 2018). Many panels and workshops stressed the urgent need to support the 2015 Paris Climate Accord to which Pope Francis has also given his strong moral support:

> While everyone has a role and responsibility to help safeguard the planet, all governments must uphold commitments agreed upon in the Paris Accord on reducing climate change. Without concerted and immediate efforts toward sustainable development, there is a real danger that we will leave future generations only rubble, deserts and refuse. We all know that much still needs to be done to implement that agreement. All governments should strive to honor the commitments made in Paris, in order to avoid the worst consequences of the climate crisis.[22]

- The Sufi mystic tradition of Islam under the leadership of Fethullah Gulen invokes the example of the medieval Sufi Masters Rumi and Ibn Arabi. Gulen's *Hizmet* (Service) movement seeks to expand our understanding of human actions in the Universe.[23] In asserting that the Universe is where God's names are manifested and that it therefore has some sort of sanctity, Gulen is echoing the views of Arabi and other Sufi sages.[24] Sadly, *Hizmet* is being persecuted by Erdogan in Turkey, but its global efforts in education are effective and influential.
- The various transformations that occurred in the life of Thomas Merton prefigure Pope Francis' sensitive ability to base his ministry on today's realities. Merton was "attuned to the reality that the world had changed considerably since he had entered Gethsemani in 1941. By the 1960's, Bob Dylan and Joan Baez were warning that 'the times they are a changing.' Western society was undergoing sociocultural turmoil caused by the sexual revolution. The monolithic Roman Catholic Church which had wooed Merton into its triumphalist ghetto was calling an end to the Constantinian era in the post Vatican II Church."[25] Merton had inspired Pope Francis on climate change—as he himself told the U. S. Congress in September, 2015.[26]
- Richard Rohr, OFM, has spearheaded a new spiritual movement which focuses on the "Universal Christ." It attempts to bridge the gaps that developed over the centuries between the human and divine natures in Jesus the Christ. Rohr presents a view of Jesus who "sets the bar for what it means to be fully human, and a Christ who is big enough to hold all of creation together in one harmonious unity."[27]

As have these four men, and as did Rachel Carson, Francis stresses that religion and science do not conflict. The pope insists on living simply. We are to reduce luxury lest our sense of justice be atrophied. One lesson to be drawn from the teachings of these glocal visionaries is that directing one's affections to comply with spiritual and ethical imperatives can prepare one to care for nature.

Warnings from the United Nations Panel and Others on Climate Change

The United Nations Intergovernmental Panel on Climate Change issued a report in October, 2018 which indicates that world leaders have only about two decades left to bring about major changes in carbon emissions to avoid worsening food shortages, more dangerous wildfires and the extinction of the coral reefs. The report "is quite a shock" and a cause for concern wrote Bill Hare, an author of previous I.P.C.C. reports and a physicist with Climate Analytics, a nonprofit organization. "We were not aware of this just a few years ago."[28] The report was the first to be commissioned by world leaders under the 2015 Paris agreement obliging nations to fight global warming. The authors found that if greenhouse gas emissions continue at the current rate, the atmosphere will warm up by as much as 2.7 degrees Fahrenheit (1.5 degrees Celsius) above preindustrial levels by 2040, inundating coastlines and intensifying droughts and poverty. Previous work had focused on estimating the damage if average temperatures were to rise by a larger number, 3.6 degrees Fahrenheit (2 degrees Celsius), because that was the threshold scientists previously considered for the most severe effects of climate change. Ignoring such warnings, the Trump administration reneged on the US commitment to the 2015 Paris Climate Accord. Most people have supported Pope Francis' warnings against climate change and his call to do whatever is possible to "escape the spiral of self-destruction which currently engulfs us."[29] In August of 2015, some Islamic leaders called for global action to offset climate change,[30] for stabilizing greenhouse gas concentration in the atmosphere at a level that would prevent dangerous anthropogenic interference with the climate systems. "Clear targets and monitoring systems are needed in view of the dire consequences[31] to planet earth if we do not do so. The present generation bears an enormous responsibility. It must find new ways to relate God's Earth and it must develop a strategy of zero emissions as early as possible." (Ibid). The Islamic leaders called on rich nations[32] and oil-producing states to lead the way in phasing out their greenhouse gas emissions as early as possible—no later than by the middle of the century.

The Ability to Foresee and Deliver on the Long-Term Needs of the Planet and Its Inhabitants

Pope Francis, as did Teilhard, realizes that interfaith understanding and harmony are essential for the future of humanity and of nature as we have known it. Both have spoken from a universal perspective. Teilhard realized that mystical experience is an essential part of most religious traditions. It is so in Sufism which has played a key role in Islam's evolution. Teilhard spent some of his formative years in Cairo, Egypt as a Jesuit scholastic. He must "have had many opportunities to encounter the Islamic faith as it was lived out in one of the historic centers of Islam. Teilhard taught Muslim students while in Cairo. He went home to the families of his Muslim students, whose warm hospitality he appreciated. He made excursions on the Nile, and visited the pyramids, Upper Egypt, Heliopolis, Memphis, and Luxor."[33]

Teilhard foresaw that traditional societies such as those of the Middle East and Africa would change in major ways as people gained access to new technologies. The Internet is now part of the daily life of many Middle East inhabitants. Teilhard felt that with technological developments people of various cultural and religious background would begin to communicate across traditional divides. New avenues of cooperation would emerge based on universal ideals such as fraternity and equality. Common needs and aspirations of the human community would eventually create new structures that would enable people of diverse backgrounds and cultures to establish new organizations linking them together. Many global NGOs have emerged within the 50 years. They assist developing nations participate in strategic planning beyond the lines of traditional nation states. In Teilhardian terms, this emergence exemplifies how convergent lines of creative efforts can function. It points toward an emergent form of religion—one that sees the world as developing dynamically. It seeks a new synthesis beyond such dichotomies as religious-secular, sacred-profane, spiritual- material, heavenly-worldly. For Teilhard, this meant that the coming era will not be one of religions as such. Rather, it is to be one laden with a new sense of religion itself. "Religion has by no means been left behind. It is only beginning."[34]

Accusations that Pope Francis is not sufficiently "Catholic" recall those who claimed that Teilhard was trying to start a new religion based on his evolutionary theory or that humanity may have outgrown traditional religious beliefs. In fact, Teilhard and Pope Francis have both taught the centrality of Jesus in world history. Both of these Jesuits were trained in empirical science, in the realities of an expanding universe. For them, scientific principles are not obstacles to faith; rather, they reinforce one another.[35] Teilhard argued that there is emerging a new form of consciousness on earth—that of the Noosphere which transcends the traditional boundaries of sectarianism, tribalism and ethnocentrism. Through his outreach to Buddhist-and-Muslim-majority nations, Pope Francis has been an exponent of such an inclusive way of being foreseen by Teilhard. He has embodied this new inclusivity through his prophetic actions. His analyses of the problems of modernity and of present ecological crises and their impact on the planet's ability to sustain projected population increases have led him to call for an integral ecology. It would balance our efforts to protect nature and to provide water, food and natural resources for all living species on earth. Francis has often spoken about how faith is related to scientific investigations. At a scientific conference in May, 2017, he spoke on how faith is related to cosmology and astronomy. He linked Big Bang theories with Teilhard's evolutionary views, telling his audience that there is no contradiction between faith in God and the prevailing scientific theories of the expanding universe. "When we read about creation in *Genesis*, we run the risk of imagining God was a magician, with a magic wand able to do everything. But that is not so," Francis said. "He created human beings and let them develop according to the internal laws that he gave to each one so they would reach their fulfillment."[36]

We conclude this chapter with an allusion to Richard Rohr's new spirituality which is an alternative to an eclecticism that uncritically dabbles with Eastern religions.[37] The "new-spirituality" views of Teilhard and of Richard Rohr (see our book's conclusion) have some parallels with blockchain technologies inasmuch as both radically re-conceptualize nature's potentialities as affected by humans.[38] Bernard Lonergan's integration of reason, faith and a glocal ethics offers us further ways to foresee and deliver on the long-term needs of planet earth and its inhabitants. The following chapter addresses some of the issues that affect the transformative roles of religion and the Church's role therein. It suggests the many glocal roles religions have played across the planet by discerning how local situations affect people's ability to accept needed change and how Pope Francis has been preparing the Church to adapt as it faces the implications. We must rely on the guidance of the Holy Spirit in our lives so that we Christians might authentically live the Good News of Jesus on all continents amidst today's complexities. But there are impediments such as a lack of comprehension by "traditional" Catholics who fail to discern what is needed to promote a glocal ethics and a glocal spirituality intent on the good of all.

Notes

1. For websites on threats of climate-change to the environment: https://catholicclimatecovenant.org/; https://greenfaith.org/?gclid=EAIaIQobChMIso788rjh4AIVAghpCh28lwOwEAAYASAAEgJkMPD_BwE#. On drug-resistant bacteria, www.betterhealth.vic.gov.au/health/conditionsandtreatments/antibiotic-resistant-bacteria

2. Henri Cardinal de Lubac, S.J., *The Religion of Teilhard de Chardin* (New York: Image Books (1967). De Lubac was one of the main authors who influenced the Vatican II document *The Church in the Modern World (Gaudium et Spes)*. De Lubac— himself censured by Pope Pius XI in 1950—was named a cardinal by Pope John Paul II in 1983.

3. To better understand Teilhard, one must recognize that his thought incorporates ideas and visions of earlier evolutionists (Lamarck, Darwin, Spencer, Nietzsche, Bergson). His scheme of evolution is grounded in four basic assumptions: spiritual monism, a cosmic law of complexity-consciousness, critical transitional thresholds, and the omega point. He has contributed to the growing holistic awareness of humankind's place in nature. See www.jstor.org/stable/23261700?seq=1#page_scan_tab_contents. Implied here is that our glocal approach to history and the papacy includes a temporal element: humanity's future depends on realistic transformations of past and present.

4. Teilhard de Chardin, *Building the Earth*. 1969. https://www.azquotes.com/quote/690346

5. The Toronto discussion touched on the teaching of *Laudato Si*'s warning (25) to humanity on this global problem and on the potential roles of religion in awakening humanity as to the impact of present climate crises.

6. We believe that Pope Francis and Teilhard have lived as glocal mystics. Both men made radical breakthroughs in their approaches to immanent-transcendent aspects of divinity as understood in both in Eastern and Western religions. "Glocal mystic" refers to those who seek insights into a universally comprehensive dimension of ultimate reality. The characters for Zen, for instance, refer to the Ultimate as being utterly simple, that is beyond words—the immanent-transcendent- apophatic Ultimate Ground of reality.

7. Teilhard de Chardin, "Hymn of the Universe. The Mass on the World." www.stmchapelhill.org/documents/2016/10/The%20Mass%20On%20The%20World.pdf. The hymn reads like a preface to a glocal mystic theology.

8   Pope John Paul II, *Gift and Mystery*, (New York: Image, 1996), 73. Teilhard and Lonergan both integrated evolutionary theory into their thinking. While Lonergan's profound treatments of human understanding and spirituality has not been censured by the Church, Teilhard was originally censured for promoting "pan psychism."
9   Joseph Cardinal Ratzinger, *Principles of Catholic Theology* (San Francisco: Ignatius Press, 1987), 334.
10 See Mary Evelyn Tucker, "Commentaries on the Pope's Message *Laudato Si*," *The Quarterly Review of Biology*, Vol. 91, 3, Sept. 2016, 269. http://fore.yale.edu/files/Integrating_Ecology_and_Justice.pdf. H. Reed Armstrong in "Teilhard de Chardin: The Vatican II Architect You Need to Know." Nov. 27, 2017. https://onepeterfive.com/ teilhard-chardin-vii-architect/ provides a context for Teilhard's contribution to Vatican II and how Pope Francis has drawn on it. The Omega Point is a spiritual belief and a scientific speculation that everything in the universe is fated to spiral towards a final point of divine unification. We interpret this as a glocal-theological viewpoint.
11 *Laudato Si*, 83. Note 53 reads "Against this horizon we can set the contribution of Fr. Teilhard de Chardin." Francis refers to earlier statements by Pope Paul VI, John Paul II and Benedict XVI in support of Teilhard.
12 Quoted in Ursula King, *Spirit of Fire: The Life and Vision of Teilhard de Chardin*. 1996, 203-04.
13 Elizabeth Kolbert's *The Sixth Extinction* studies how humans affect the environment. She concludes that we are close to the sixth extinction in the planet's history. The ability to sustain future population growth is now threatened. A glocal "integral ecology" would ensure a balance between efforts to protect nature and sustaining all living species. We are in drastic need of glocal environmental policies. See, for example, www.cambridge.org/core/ journals/british-journal-of-political-science/ article/all-policies-are-glocal-international-environmental-policy-making-with-strategic-subnational-governments/87BCCDE56859945E9549B5716500B0BC
14 In June 2019, the pope told oil executives that there is not time to lose on the crisis of climate change. https://www.leonardodicaprio.org/pope-francis-to-oil-executives-no-time-to-lose-on-climate-change/
15 http://reference.bahai.org/en/t/je/BNE/bne-166.html, 209.
16 Ursula King, *Teilhard de Chardin and Eastern Religions* (2011), 230. "Animation" is crucial in pastoral practice.

17 Rafal Serafin, "Vernadsky's Biosphere, Teilhard's Noosphere, and Lovelock's Gaia: Perspectives on Human Intervention in Global Biogeochemical Cycles," http://pure.iiasa.ac.at/id/eprint/2956/. Our ability to interact with the global conscious and thus get closer to God is labeled "hypertextuality" in Jean-Nicholas Bazin's *Virtual Christianity*. Hypertext connects all pieces of information on the internet. There is no piece of information without context. Text is devalued in favor of context. Interactive, hypertextual content is preferred over simple textual content. Hypertext threatens and flattens hierarchies. Social media allowed protesters in the middle east to organize in a new way, thus enabling the Arab Spring. See https://urloved.com/2016/06/08/the-glocal-church/ The internet could do the same for God's mission in the World. For an example of how some paradigm shifts are influencing leading in mission, see Kirk Franklin, "Leading in Global-Glocal Missional Contexts: Learning from the Journey of the Wycliffe Global Alliance" https://journals.sagepub.com/doi/abs/10.1177/0265378817724343.

"Since Christianity is both an agent and product of globalization, its beliefs have spread from one source to another, crossing religious, linguistic and cultural contexts. As a result, there are polycentric or multiple centers of influence since Christianity has homes within a diversity of contexts. This carries with it various implications including how partnering in mission needs to be deconceptualized through greater emphasis on friendship. In order for this to happen as a missiological principle, third spaces may need to be created. Viewed against the backdrop of church and mission agency leadership, structures may be 'stuck in the Industrial Era' (Complexity Leadership Theory Uhl-Bien et al., 2007: 298). The stage is now set for exploring how these and other themes influence approaches to God's mission.

18 Since the 1990s, glocalization has been well thematized by some social scientists. It is the "simultaneous occurrence of both universalizing and particularizing. Glocal, an adjective, by definition, is "reflecting or characterized by both local and global. The term entered into English via Robertson in the teaching of culture, information, morality, spirituality, religion, etc. through Canadian sociologists Keith Hampton and Barry Wellman, among others. See Victor Roudometof, Glocalization: A Critical Introduction (New York: Routledge, 2016).

19 He reportedly anticipated the Internet and a possible singularity. See www.vice.com/en_us/article/nz7z7q/the-priest-who-believed-in-god-and-the-singularity-pierre-teilhard-de-chardin

20 https://w2.vatican.va/content/john-paul-ii/en/audiences/2001/documents/hf_jp-ii_aud_20010117.html
21 Cristina Vanin, www.kings.uwo.ca/ kings/assets/ File/ academics/ centres/carct/Glocal-Theology.pdf
22 "Pope Francis calls on world governments to uphold Paris climate accords" *America*. July 6, 2018. See also www.worldwildlife.org/stories/us-climate-action-grows-stronger-despite-announcement-to-leave-paris-agreement
23 https://fgulen.com/en/home/1359-fgulen-com-english/gulens-works/recent-articles/24770-the-meaning-of-life
24 Gerald Grudzen, "The Divine Imprint in Nature: Fethullah Gulen and Teilhard de Chardin." *Omega: The Indian Journal of Science and Religion*. December, 2016, 152.
25 www.irishtimes.com/culture/books/thomas-merton-the-hermit-who-never-was-his-young-lover-and-mysterious-death-1.2422818 Merton found it hard to adapt himself to his twin interest as monk and social activist.
26 Nick Fouriezos, www.ozy.com/flashback/the-environmentalist-monk-who-inspired-pope-francis/67179
27 Rohr, *The Universal Christ, How a Forgotten Reality Can Change Everything We See* (Convergent, 2019), 106. For Rohr, history is both evolutionary and positive. He finds confirmation in Jesus' many parables of the Kingdom. Rohr holds up Merton's ontological spirituality, based on a non-dual consciousness, that "rejects the splits of dualistic thinking. . . .. One must see God in Everything." *National Catholic Reporter*, Dec. 28, 2018-Jan. 10, 2019, 7.
28 *New York Times*, October 7, 2018. www.nytimes.com/2018/10/07/climate/ipcc-climate-report-2040.html. On a study that came to similar conclusions, John Raymaker with Ijaz Durrani, *Empowering Climate-Change Strategies with Bernard Lonergan's Method* (Lanham, MD, UPA, 2015). Humanity is *not* on the path of avoiding "the most dangerous aspects of climate change." The probability of "near-term" extinctions of species is now real. (68).
29 https://rlp.hds.harvard.edu/files/hds-rlp/files/ climate_change_christianity.pdf. *Laudato Si* influenced the 2015 Paris Climate Accord. It was rumored that the pope made personal phone calls to some Catholic representatives.
30 *Declaration on Climate Change*, August 2015. https://unfccc.int/news/islamic-declara"tion-on-climate-change.

31 See https://truthout.org/articles/ the-insect-apocalypse-is- coming-here-are-five-lessons- we-must-learn/
32 The world's richest countries are full of anxious, alienated People: William Horobin, www.bloomberg.com/ news/articles/2019-03-19/rich-countries-welfare-spending-leaves-people-wanting-more
33 Ursula King, *The Life and Vision of Teilhard de Chardin.* (New York: Orbis, 1996) 2.
34 Ursula King. *Teilhard de Chardin and Eastern Religions*, 169. She has focused on Teilhard's "zest for life."
35 *Encyclopedia of Time: Science, Philosophy, Theology, & Culture*, Volume 1, 434. Sage Publications, 2009.
36 *The Washington Post.* "Pope Says Evolution is Real, and God is no Wizard." December 28, 2014.
37 Our glocal holistic spirituality differs from Fritjof Capra's eclectic New Age views in his *The Tao of Physics.*
38 George Gilder, author of *Life After Google*, argues that blockchain technology is revolutionizing the Internet. He has commented on some of the breakthrough research of Carver Mead. www.youtube.com/watch?v=Mz91ZEr6IZQ

PART TWO
The Transformative Roles of Religion Across the Planet

CHAPTER 4
Transitional Glocal Issues

This chapter on transitional issues considers aspects of what a glocal Church implies.[1] Chapters 5-7 explore the *global* implications of the Church's mission. Part Three will consider some *local* issues. Our glocal (global-local) focus is our way of specifying how Pope Francis is building "bridges of fraternity."[2] His glocal-relational theology seeks to resolve the tensions afflicting humanity. As part of our efforts to link the roots of religion, spirituality, science and ethics, we first recall[3] the gifted teacher, Anne Sullivan, known for her work with Helen Keller, a blind and deaf child whom she taught to communicate with others. Sullivan's parents had immigrated to the United States from Ireland during the Great Famine of the 1840s. A strong-willed Catholic from a humble background, she has been portrayed by some twenty actresses. Her devotion to Keller, personifies what it is to be a spiritual leaven as taught by Jesus. Amidst today's complexities, it is important to be a spiritual leaven that bears fruit. God works in hidden ways in our lives. It is in this spirit that we touch on Buddhism and Islam as treated by Thomas Merton and others. Living with members of other religions and their different ethical views is part and parcel of the complexities that a book on glocal-prophetic dialogue cannot avoid as its seeks to assess and develop Pope Francis' novel ways of spiritual bridge-building and of enlightening us glocally.

Unresolved Problems Confronting Humanity in Need of Glocal Solutions[4]

How does living in a digitalized-glocalized world affect the churches today? As Sullivan and Keller had a life-long partnership for dealing with blindness, so we seek enlightenment. How be enlightened when a witch's brew of claims have led to such tragic events as the Afghanistan and Iraq wars—both based on miscalculations? William Bush Jr.'s false "weapons-of-mass-destruction" claims had catastrophic consequences in Iraq—as have Russian and Western interventions in Afghanistan. At the root of such tragedies lies human blindness to the deeper spiritual-ethical issues we are examining. Opposition to Pope Francis is often a matter of the blind leading the blind, as when rich Catholics, intent on profiting,[5] fail to see that the pope is calling us to live Jesus' Good News in simple, caring ways, or when liberal Catholics are blinded to the pope's insistence on holiness. In fact, the pope upholds the traditional Catholic values but is updating them to fit the demands of a complex world. In many ways, he is doing for today's Church what St. Paul did some 2,000 years ago. Saul, a Jewish zealot, changed from persecuting Christians after being blinded on his way to Damascus. He then began preaching Jesus as the Light of the World. Pope Francis is now asking Christians to do the same. St. Paul's role in establishing Christianity was an early glocal breakthrough: he adapted his message of universal salvation to fit the concrete realities of the audiences he was addressing. Notable differences are that Pope Francis must *administer* a glocal Church in a divided world often victimized by flows of "instantaneous" fake news.

From Saint Paul, the Visionary[6] Apostle, to Present Interfaith Realities

By the middle of the first century, the Christian community had to address a key problem. The questions raised at the Council of Jerusalem and the conflicts within the fledging faith communities in Antioch,[7] (such as the status of Gentile converts) led St. Paul to undertake his missionary journeys. His vision was much less apocalyptic than that found in the *Book of Revelation*. He believed that Christ was the first born of a new creation. He based his preaching on the visionary experience he had of the risen Christ: "I was given the knowledge of the mystery, as I have described it .... If you read my words, you will have some idea of the depths that I see in the mystery of Christ. (*Ephesians* 3:1-3). In *Galatians*, St. Paul describes this in simple words pregnant with meaning: "It pleased him, to reveal His Son in me that I might preach Him among the Gentiles. (1:15-16). St. Paul focuses on "revelation, sonship, and preaching to the Gentiles."[8] Having experienced the power of the mystery of Christ, he was impelled to share the mystery with all those who would hear him. Pope Francis walks in the steps of St. Paul—helping us better follow Christ in "glocally conscienticizing" ways[9] and by helping humans face impending tasks.

The world religions—Buddhism, Christianity and Islam—are "glocal religions" in contrast to Hinduism and Judaism. Buddhism has its roots in Hinduism; Christianity and Islam have theirs in Judaism. While the world glocal religions concern themselves with all cultures, with all inhabitants of the earth, Hinduism and Judaism mostly confine themselves within the cultural, religious heritage of their own ancestors.[10] The three world religions have recently been cooperating in glocal ways—as has been occurring in The World Parliament of Religions. Glocal cooperation has been growing due to the ever-increasing number of "contact zones" on the globe, permitting humans of multitudinous backgrounds to interact with one another on a daily basis. Historically, the beliefs of Christians were disputed by the Prophet Muhammad. Sadly, the differing views of Christians and Muslims have been and still are among the chief reasons for instability and wars in the world.[11] Partly underlying the global conflicts that have occurred since the death of Muhammad is the split among the Sunni and Shiite versions of Islam. Just as the three religions of the Book (Judaism, Christianity, and Islam) are divided in their interpretations of their scriptures, so is Buddhism. The practices of Theravada, the original form of Buddhism, differ significantly from those of Mahayana in East Asia.[12] As opposed to having a global perspective on the world, most people are absorbed in their own local situations. They cannot fully grasp the scope of global needs. The one, holy, catholic, apostolic Church received its mission from Christ. Pope Francis is the conscience of the world who seeks to bridge gaps in religion and politics. As were St. Paul and St. Francis, he is a mystic-in-action[13] able to relate his inner life to the outer world's needs.

Glocal-Mystical Underpinnings That Help Us Interrelate Our Inner and Outer Lives

Being a glocal Church[14] implies building bridges between global and local concerns. A task of the Church is to help people live spiritual lives. The word "religion" is derived from the Latin *ligare*, "to bind." Religion, as binding us to God, should also bind humans together. But this has often not been the case. Surely, in our age when we humans endanger the planet itself, we must unite—whether we be religious, secularist or atheist. Influenced by Teilhard, Jean Houston argues that "We live in a time in which more and more history is happening faster and faster than we can make sense of. The habits of millennia seem to vanish in a few months and the convictions of centuries are crashing down. And yet, the deconstruction of traditional ways of being may invite the underlying Spirit"[15] to break through. She adds: "Many have written of the mystic path and tracked its myriad adventures and planes of development. The mystic path is predicated on awakening, on . . . abandoning lackluster passivity to engage co-creation with vigor, attention, focus, and radiance, characteristics we might note we often find in our animal friends." (Ibid.) Houston has been influenced by

Evelyn Underhill's *Mysticism* (1911) which "presents the mystic path as a series of eight organic stages: awakening, purification, illumination, voices and visions, contemplation and introversion, ecstasy and rapture, the dark night of the soul, and union with the One Reality." (Ibid). In the first stage, "awakening," one wakes up, to put it quite simply. Suddenly, the world is filled with splendor and glory, and one understands that one is a citizen in a much larger universe. One is filled with the awareness that one is a part of an enormous Life, in which everything is connected to everything else."[16] In the final eighth stage of "'unitive life," one exists in the state of union with the One Reality — experiencing a Oneness with God:

> For those who enter this state, it seems as if nothing is impossible. They become world changers and world servers. They become powers for life, centers for energy, partners and guides for spiritual vitality in other human beings. They glow, and they set others glowing. They are force fields, and to be in their fields is to be set glowing. They are no longer human beings as we have known them. They are fields of being, for they have moved from Godseed to Godself. (Ibid).

Mystic Experiences and Dealing with the Threats of Both Psychic and Environmental Collapse

With Pope Francis, we seek to build bridges in a world threatened by environmental collapse, one in which collective fantasies play their roles. Fortunately, psychic and mystical experiences *can* help us live sound lives in a glocalized world. Such experiences—if genuine and realistic—can help interrelate persons to one another on a sound basis. Daniel Helminiak, a psychologist, has written on the current debate over the capacity of the human brain to experience God. He seeks to resolve the mind-body problem by clarifying the nature of human consciousness. He shows how Bernard Lonergan's thought applies to both physical and non-physical realities. This double-application potential is helpful in relating psychology, spirituality, theology and neuroscience in ways that coalesce in explaining our experiences of the transcendent. Unlike neuroscience, psychology addresses the mind as a distinct reality, governed by its own laws and capable of distinctive acts: self-aware imagery, emotions, memories, insight, choice. Our minds can have both psychic and a transcendent experiences. The latter touch on the spiritual. With repetition, such experiences occur ever more easily because of a person's ongoing accommodation "to the open-ended dynamism of the human spirit. There occurs a concomitant restructuring of the neurological base of the psyche and, then, of the human spirit."[17] Although one cannot reason with the insane or deranged, psychotherapists are called to heal deep wounds. People want to cling to what makes them feel comfortable and safe; they are afraid of changing course. Yes, discussion and sharing do help, but the issues are complicated as they are deeply intertwined within one's psyche and in centuries-old traditions. To give them up poses an intolerable existential threat, the collapse of one's world. We may extend Helminiak's argument to the threatening collapse of the environment. In neither case, can we expect God to pull strings to solve threats. Recall that a Gordian Knot refers to a problem solvable only by bold action. Pope Francis is asking us to act boldly on climate change. Since we have mismanaged the environment, we must now take countervailing measures.[18] Helminiak's insights into how the Creator may be operating deep within our human psyches points to a need for glocal psychologies.

Comparing the Addresses of Pope Benedict XVI and of Pope Francis to Muslims

A glocal psychology or its lack may be illustrated by two of Pope Benedict's speeches to Muslims. The first touches on his inept remarks in Regensburg in 2006 that damaged Christian-Islamic relations. There, he quoted a 14th century dialogue between a Persian and the Byzantine emperor. The emperor had provocatively said: "Show me just what Muhammad brought that was new, and there you will find things only evil and inhuman, such as his command to spread by the sword the faith he preached."[19] This statement sparked much controversy and violence on the part of Muslims. Actually, the Regensburg speech was not about Islam. His 4,500-word address devoted a mere three paragraphs to the emperor's remark. He had used it to set up his reflections on his chosen topic, which was "Faith, Reason and the University." What he was trying to do is to chide Westerners' conduct now sunk into a relativism bereft of true values! He wanted to stress how important it is that religion never part company with reason. He could just as easily have taken his cautionary tale from Hinduism, Buddhism, or Christianity. Benedict's real target in the speech was the West. He was trying to identify two worrying trends in Western thought –one inside the Christian church, and the other in the broader culture. The full version of his speech traced the historical efforts to situate the use of ancient Greek concepts of reason in the early Church. Greek concepts were an historical accident—not essential to Christian faith. But Benedict added that it was providential that the Biblical faith and Greek thought had intersected for it enabled Christians to recognize that reason is intrinsic to God's nature. To act irrationally is to break with God's will. Benedict was even more critical of trends in Western culture that regard only the so-called "hard sciences" as truly rational or objective. To relegate everything else - including morality - to the realm of personal preference and choice is a perversion.

A more propitious approach to Islam by Pope Benedict had occurred in 2005 in Cologne, when he met with local leaders of the Muslim community. In that address, he said, "Interreligious and intercultural dialogue between Christians and Muslims cannot be reduced to an optional extra. It is in fact a vital necessity, on which in large measure our future depends."[20] In 2005, Pope Benedict was more conscious of the need for glocal psychologies to underpin Christian-Muslim relations. Pope Francis' promotion of interfaith dialogue is based on his realization that global conflicts are rooted in misunderstandings and a lack of communication among religious leaders.[21] He ably appeals to adequate glocal psychologies. Since 2013, he and the churches of the Middle-East have engaged in Christian-Islamic dialogue to help forestall jihadists. While he was in Cairo in 2017, he met with Tawadros II, head of the Coptic Orthodox Church.[22] He embraced the Grand Imam of Al-Azhar mosque, Sheikh Ahmed el-Tayeb. The embrace echoed St. Francis of Assisi's mission to Islamic leader Sultan Al-Kamil 800 years ago. For his part, Grand Imam el-Tayeb stressed the need for the Muslim-majority nations to welcome Christians. To Muslims he said: "Continue to embrace" Christian citizens "since they are your partners". He told Christians, "You are citizens with full rights and responsibilities."[23] Such Christian-bridge-building activities are signs that moderate Muslims and Christians in the Middle East can live together in mutually-enhancing ways.[24] Pope Francis' efforts in this area are further illustrated in his other visits to other moderate Muslim-majority countries such as Morocco, Bangladesh, and the United Arab Republic. He is willing to "cross over to the other side." His outreach to Muslims had already begun Argentina when he was the first Catholic bishop to visit an Islamic Center in that country.

Pope Francis Has Aptly Addressed Thomas Merton's Glocal-Mystical Insights

In Pope Francis' speech before the U. S. Congress in 2015, Thomas Merton was one of four Americans he praised. He cited Merton's description of himself in *The Seven Story Mountain*, as a man born in freedom, but a prisoner of his own selfishness who did manage to overcome the contradictions of life all humans face. "He became a man of prayer and thought that led to his becoming a voice for dialogue between religions and between enemy nations."[25] The pope praised Merton's bridge-building ability: "The work of building bridges between enemies requires courage and daring." (Ibid). Good political leaders prefer to work for peace rather than occupy a country. Francis strongly denounced the arms race and its monetary goals. Merton pioneered paths for Christian-Muslim dialogues. In an age of resurgent radical Islam, it is clear that any real understanding of Islam includes grasping how Islam's message is being falsified by extremists. So we have to "dig deeper" into the religious realities experienced by mystics such as Merton. Merton was deeply interested in Islam long before today's terrorist attacks. This was due to his interest in Sufism as well as in Buddhism. Buddhist, Christian, and Islamic mystics share a common trait: that of going beyond words. All of them seek to experience a glimpse of ultimate reality as it were. It involves a grasping for an apprehension that transcends the mundane—reaching for the realm of inexpressible reality, the realm of heart-to-heart relations with God, with ultimate reality.

The glocal mystic Merton was, and remained, a Christian. Yet his studies of Buddhism and Islam and his correspondence with representatives of both faiths gave him many insights into the deep life of prayer that God makes available to all humans seeking the Divine.[26] His studies of Islam focused on its central concepts such as the unity of God (*tawhid*) and the "sending down" (revelation-*tanzil*) of God's word. But his real fascination was with spiritual realities, the way in which Islam, as Merton put it, set people 'free to travel in a realm of white-hot faith as bare and grand as the desert itself."[27] For Merton, "the basic thing in Islam is that man should come to know Allah by his name. The basic "facts of the religion," the "sending down" of the Holy *Qur'an* to the Prophet Muhammad, the Five Pillars of Islam, the law (*sharia*), are all gifts of God, ways God attempts to make the Divine Self known to creation.[28] One of the poems that Merton wrote about Islam is called "The Night of Destiny" which refers to the night when Muslims believe that Muhammad received his first revelation. His poem is about the coming of the "Word." It begins and ends with the T.S. Eliot-esque line, "in my ending is my meaning." In the poem the speaker seems to be reading at night by a lamp, a "Weak friend/In the knowing night." (Ibid), But he is, in fact, illuminated by the "tongue of flame/Under the heart," an image from Sufi literature. The poem asks,

"Who holds the homeless light secure/In the deep heart's room?" The enigmatic, but precise answer is "Midnight! Kissed with flame!" Life, interior life, is mysterious and may be dark ("love is black"), but there are fleeting moments of illumination, of being kissed by love (another Sufi notion). All of the images of darkness in the poem are positive. Night is "knowing," love is "darkness" but a lamp does provide "the small circle of seeing." Midnight is "kissed with flame," and in the night all the lost are found. God is inscrutable, but Benevolent and Merciful (*rahman* and *rahim*). The speaker of the poem exclaims, "My love is darkness!" and closes in the "void" where all ways are one and "all the lost" are found. In the "void" or "emptiness" of the inscrutable love of God, Christianity and Islam embrace." Ibid. The reasons for this embrace was profoundly Christian. In a letter to Abdul Aziz on June 2, 1963, Merton says, "We must strive more and more to be universal in our interests and in our zeal of the glory of the one God, and may His Name be magnified in us."[29] The Christian's universal embrace reflects the nature of the God of Christians Who, as Jesus taught, stands in the road waiting to embrace those who come home. While it would be comforting to hold this view, Michael Ford, noting Islamic conflicts, argues that Merton's later remarks to Abdul Aziz on November 7, 1965 are an appropriate and timely conclusion:

> Well, my friend, we live in troubled and sad times, and we must pray the infinite and merciful Lord to bear patiently with the sins of this world . . . . We must humble our hearts in silence and in poverty of spirit and listen to His commands which come from the depths of His love and work that men's hearts may be converted to the ways of love and justice, not of blood, murder, lust and greed. I am afraid that . . . powerful countries are a bad example to the rest of the world in this respect. (Ibid).

Linking the Roots of Religion and Spirituality with Science and Glocal Forms of Ethics

There are now Catholic Zen masters in the West. In Japan, Ichiro Okumura, a Carmelite priest, wrote an inspiring book, *Awakening to Prayer*, in which he explores the roots of prayer as a divine-human divine reality. He draws on the insights of Eastern and Western spiritual traditions. Prayer is a conversation: one listens and rests in the divine.[30] St. Francis witnessed the transition from the "Dark Ages" to the Middle Ages. In our age of omnipresent cellphones, glocal consciousness is a reality. Traditionally, missionaries have always had to face glocal issues, but not enough of them realized they were helping colonialism. In the 13th century, the Franciscan and Dominican Orders helped evangelize the Middle East and portions of Andalusia that would become the nation of Spain. By the 16th century, Spain, Portugal and France had begun colonizing the Americas. Franciscans and Dominicans evangelized the indigenous populations. Unfortunately, St. Francis' ecological mysticism and the intellectual synthesis of Thomistic metaphysics and theology became intertwined with the Catholic Church's growing rigidity and with the Inquisition.

Christians have always been taught to accept God's hidden doings. But evil is an ever-present reality as Joseph Conrad pointed out. Today, we humans seem bent on destroying the planet. This sad fact recalls Schweitzer's words: "Man has lost the capacity to foresee."[31] There is much we can now learn from the indigenous wisdom which the West strove to obliterate. Pope Francis stresses that this was a gross injustice.[32] The traditional and modern forms of religion and morality are quite complex; they are part and parcel of the complexities that a book on glocal-prophetic dialogue must not overlook. By way of addressing such complexities, the rest of this chapter interlinks various issues affecting the Church. We shall ask 1) How might digitalization promote the common glocal good? 2) How can traditional forms of Islamic and Asian spiritualities help Westerners in their quest? 3) How can modern spiritualities nourish the Church today? 4) Why has the pope's ability to address many-faceted realities confused, or even antagonized his critics? In answer to the latter, we suggest that Francis' revising the notion of collegiality and his prioritizing preaching the Good News of Jesus has been misunderstood by his critics.

1) How Might Digitalization Promote the Common Glocal Good?

Sadly, many Christians fail to live gospel priorities, to love neighbor as one's self. Rooted in history and directed toward a future based on mutual tolerance, with Pope Francis, we have set out on a journey that requires us to contrast the priorities of the good news of Jesus' gospel with those of the world. As Jesus reached out to the despised Samaritans of his day, so we seek to foster believers' outreach to today's many victims of injustice. For this purpose, it may be well to recall a few texts from St. Matthew touching on Jesus' core teachings: on being peacemakers (Matt 5:9); on the need of letting the seed sown in our hearts sink deeply; on the Kingdom of God being like a yeast that a woman took and hid in three measures of flour till it was all leavened," Matt 13:33. As yeast is a one-celled organism that produces carbohydrates causing a bread to rise, so we seek to recall Christians to core gospel values.

So as to better confront Christian failures to live the message of Jesus, we explore the spiritual writings of Buddhist, Christian and Islamic mystics. We do so in the interest of a deeper glocal spirituality—one that may partly obviate Schweitzer's felt need to reject liberal theology. In the "Our Father" we pray "Thy Kingdom come." Humans are God's creatures—a reality the various religions answer in their own ways. Pioneers in interfaith dialogue such as Panikkar, Jacques Dupuis,[33] Bede Griffiths and Thomas Merton have written about how religions may be united in faith but separated by their beliefs. True faith is rooted in an ethical practice of justice. Interfaith dialogue must be based on self-transcendent reciprocity.[34] We agree with Victor Frankl's statement in *Man's Search for Meaning*, 1967, that "The true meaning of life is to be discovered in the world rather than within man or his own psyche, as though it were a closed system" (126). The self-transcendence of human existence means that being human always "is directed, to something or someone, other than oneself—be it a meaning to fulfill or another human being to encounter. The more one forgets "one's self by giving self to a cause to serve or another person to love—the more human," he/she is. What is called self-actualization is not directly attainable "for the simple reason that the more one would strive for it," the more he/she misses it. Self-actualization is possible only as a side-effect of self-transcendence." (Ibid). Healthy forms of glocalization are those that help people become conscious of inherent complexities. As Pope Francis travels the world, meeting with diverse people, his smiles show that he is not afraid to face complexities.

2) How Can Sound Traditional Buddhist-Christian-Islamic Spiritualities Help Christians in Their Quest?

In dealing with Christian-Islamic forms of mystic love-in-action for the good of all, it is important to stress the faith-belief distinction originally made by William Cantwell Smith and endorsed by Bernard Lonergan. Faith, an eye of love,[35] can unite believers; beliefs in particular doctrines tend to divide believers. All too many Christians have cut themselves off from the faith, (from God) due to false beliefs. But despite the fact that religious answers differ, there is a common, salutary tendency among reflective persons to ask themselves what led them, to the question of God, of ultimate reality, to a quest for a hopefully unitive faith.[36] Writing with a broad stroke of the pen, one might characterize Buddhist convictions as a way of exploring true reality (*dharma*) in ways that yield insights into the "ungenerated" whole.[37] In our view, traditional Buddhist-Christian-Islamic spiritualities are all efforts of a glocal eye of love—variously expressed in the beliefs of the world's religions. Unfortunately, differences in religious expression have caused, and still cause tensions and conflicts. Some believers of different religions, hoping to put aside disagreements, are participating in efforts to end violent terrorism. Violence cannot per se be attributed to religions; it is due to other causes. The faith-belief distinction helps promote glocal love by differentiating between such a love and verbal beliefs. Faith transcends but does not negate the beliefs expressed in dogmas (Lonergan, ibid, 119). As an archetypal ground of human consciousness, faith enters one's life wrapped in Mystery. In the realm of faith, love precedes knowledge. Faith, *as an inner eye of love*, has motivated persons to live heroic lives: it penetrates beneath the surface of life's sordid aspects. It helps unify religious people. Beliefs tend to divide since words cannot do justice to the mysteries of faith even though they play an indispensable role in speaking with "congregations" of believers. This point is best illustrated in the fact that Islam rejects Christian belief in the Mystery of the Holy Trinity. Muhammad insisted that there is "No God but Allah." That chasm can only partly be bridged by a mystical faith, an eye of love, that tolerates different beliefs.[38] Christians and Muslims have their own beliefs underpinned by a faith in the Creator. Atheist secularists, too, have beliefs—which they cannot prove. In the light of these realities, a faith-based glocal mystic vision can help unite humans rather than divide them. The various mystic traditions of Buddhism, Christianity and Islam can all be of help here.

Life and the universe are replete with mystery beyond thought or expectation. This is also exemplified by the "Unitarian Universalist Mystics in Community" group which believes "that the direct experience of transcending mystery and wonder is a wellspring for a life of faith.....A deeper spiritual awareness can open us to the forces that create and uphold life."[39] Our glocal worldview[40] avoids relativism. It does recognize the need and right of the three world religions to stand by their beliefs but asks them to be open to a faith strategy that can lead to needed collaboration on the world scene. This is where the beliefs of the several religions, when informed by an apophatic[41] mysticism, can play crucial roles.

Although Bevans and Schroeder touch on the importance of mysticism in prophetic dialogue, they do not draw the full implications of how a faith-belief distinction can help. Faith's eye of love is needed to bridge belief variations. "Glocal eyes" of love reflect a path of spiritual attainment inspired by the founders of the three major world religions and lived, by such renowned Islamic Sufi mystics[42] as Abu Hamid al-Ghazali (1058-1111 CE) and Rumi (1207-1271). These two Sufis, as well as Carmelite mystics and Pope Francis have stressed God's mercy in our lives. For William Chittick, God "has no choice because mercy pertains to the very stuff of reality. He cannot give priority to wrath over mercy, to severity over gentleness, because that would be to give priority to unreality over reality, ... to others rather than to himself. It would contradict the truth upon which the universe is built, the fact that there is no reality but God, there is no true existence but God's existence.[43] Faith reaches out to all[44] as exemplified by Mother Teresa and her devoted orders of missionary sisters and brothers of charity.

3) How Can Diverse Modern Spiritualities Nourish Authentic Ways of Being Church Today?

Marianne Farina has written on "sacred conversations" and on the evolution of dialogue illustrating how religions and cultures have encountered one another in varying global contexts fostering "a deep learning about God.[45] Sacred conversations honor the integrity of all religious traditions despite some syncretistic tendencies in their teachings and practices. The common ground of faith becomes a shared experience of witnessing to God's transformational action in a believer's life. Such interfaith encounters manifest the holiness of persons and faith communities striving to live faith authentically. (Ibid) How can sacred conversations be framed in realistic contexts[46] in a world in which in the past decade there have emerged such authoritarian politicians as Trump in the United States, Putin in Russia, Xi in China, Erdogan in Turkey, Orban in Hungary, Duterte in the Philippines—just to cite some prominent examples? Orwellian fake news and various types of strong-armed actions are all too much in evidence. Against such *Realpolitik* scenarios, Pope Francis has named an increasing number of cardinals from the Third World. Some developing countries which never had had a cardinal now have one. Among the pope's choices for cardinal in 2014 was Archbishop Quevedo of Cotabato in the Philippines). Quevedo had become "the chief living intellectual architect of the pastoral ideas coming out the of the Federation of Asian Bishops' Conference." [47] This Conference has distinguished itself with its vision of a church "centered on the ideal of the local church as the primary ecclesial unity." (Ibid). In effect, this vision[48] matches that of Pope Francis. It is a vision which reaches back into the early history of the Church when theologians first began to ask whether local churches are mere "franchises" as it were of the universal ministry of the pope. The New Testament uses *"ecclesia"* to refer to local self-governing churches, but this use was later expanded to include the Universal Church. Pope Francis and Quevedo have both wanted to make sure that the original emphasis on the local church not be overlooked. Quevedo's writings have led to the Asian bishops promoting their own vision of being church in modern times. It is a vision built on what the Asian bishops call the "triple dialogue," namely "a church in dialogue with local cultures, with local religions and with the local poor who make up most of Asia. Is such a vision that of "rebel" bishops or of a "rebel pope"? No! "It is one that seeks input, innovation and dialogue,"[49] from local churches; it respects local cultures for without such a respect the Christian message will fall on deaf ears. A further implication of Quevedo's being named cardinal is that he has been a close colleague and mentor to the younger Manila Cardinal Luis Antonio Tagle. Tagle, a specialist in ecclesiology, is now touted as a strong candidate to succeed Francis. If indeed Francis' successor were to come from the Third world, new transforming synergies for proclaiming the Good News of Jesus in our age of uncertainties and for dialoguing with the world's main religions are almost sure to emerge.

4) Why Does Pope Francis' Ability to Address Complex Realities Confuse—Even Antagonize His Critics?

Two years after he became pope, the German periodical, *Der Spiegel*, wrote that many had begun to wonder[50] whether Francis could, in fact, update the Church.[51] He had helped the poor inasmuch as he could. He had straightened out the Vatican Bank's finances. But he had also "created confusion in the Curia." He had negotiated between Cuba and the United States, but also scared the Israelis by calling Palestinian President Mahmoud Abbas an "angel of peace." For some, Francis is an "enigmatic problem." What is his overarching plan? Many seemed to agree "that the pope is a troublemaker. Like a billiard player who nudges the balls and calmly studies the collisions, Francis is getting things rolling in the Vatican. His interest in experimentation may stem from his study of chemical engineering. He makes decisions like Jesuit leaders— after thorough consultation, but ultimately on his own."

(Ibid). The *Spiegel* stresses that the pope decides on the basis of collegiality. In our words, he is teaching the Church to start deciding in glocally-sensitive ways—hoping to enlarge people's vision. But how? Francis's way of building bridges in a glocalized world calls for a decentralized church, for revising church structures. It is to be based on collegiality, on synodal consultations—two of the central themes stemming from the Vatican II Council. Catholic conservatives[52] often argue against collegiality. By appointing Quevedo, a proponent of collegiality, as cardinal, the pope was reiterating his own vision of being Church today. It is a vision which can help us reconcile notions of the sacred and the secular in our lives.[53] We can put this in perspective by relating the pope's vision with the key Buddhist insight that "all is interrelated."[54] The interrelatedness of all can help ground the notion of prophetic dialogue by way of the faith-belief distinction. Faith, as lived by mystics of all religions, is an eye of love that can help unite humans. The writings of mystics furnish a common ground which provides deeper foundations for renewing the Church. Practically-speaking, the pope reaches back to Jesus himself and his Good News, by engaging in prophetic dialogue and by renewing the church through forms of collegiality. The import of his initiatives are misunderstood by his critics who somehow feel threatened in their beliefs. What is important is living the faith on Jesus's terms. We argue that the pope exemplifies[55] "a needed way of being Church."

As noted earlier, anthropologists now study culture as sets of highly interrelated, heterogeneous symbols. Culture helps us understand why nations use differing norms in their conduct.[56] Tragically, anti-democratic forces have sprung up; they impair democratic principles. Since the Ukraine Orange Revolution (2004) and the Arab Spring (2010-2011), rulers have demonized democratic principles. The passage of an Anti-Foreign NGO law in Hungary (2017) is modelled on one passed in Russia in 2012. Both laws require NGOs receiving foreign funding to register as "foreign agents." Trump demonizes his critics. Pope Francis opposes these autocratic trends. A Glocal Church needs spiritual-ethical foundations. The pope's outreach to the marginalized and to other religions is based on such glocal foundations.

Robert Mickens alleges that the Church is "imploding" [57] due to its anachronistic structure. Important decisions are made by celibate clerics with little or no accountability; this must change. The Vatican Leaks scandal exposing the private papers of Benedict XVI caused deep embarrassment to him and his top aides. Pope Francis seems determined to change present structures[58] by implementing the principles outlined in *Joy of the Gospel*—his vision and blueprint for Church renewal. Francis embodies a *Kairos* (a providential moment). He is "effectively laying the foundation for the 'deconstruction' of the current Church model by patiently planting the seeds for the Church's structural conversion by 'baptizing' and employing four, key sociological principles outlined in no. 222-37 of *Joy of the Gospel*, as well as collegiality." (Ibid) We argue with the pope that a glocal collegiality is a solid ground not only for renewing the Church and for ensuring ecclesial unity in our age, but also for undertaking broad forms of needed dialogue across the globe as suggested in the following three chapters.

Notes

1 Eric Célérier, "To be relevant for our generation, we need to be glocal in our approach." "The Church as Glocal: Addressing the World and Our Community." www.lausanneworldpulse.com/themedarticles-php/1281/05-2010. On the shift in global Catholic population: www.pewforum.org/2013/02/13/the-global-catholic-population/
2 In his message, "A Critical Time for Bridge-Building, Catholic Theological Ethics Today" (July, 2018), the pope encouraged ethicists "to be passionate about dialogue," to build bridges so as to remove walls dividing humans.
3 We might also recall the heroic work of Dorothy Day (1897-1980), a Catholic convert. As part of the Catholic Worker Movement, Day co-founded the *Catholic Worker* newspaper in 1933, and served as its editor until her death. She and Frederick Franck, founder of the *Pacem in Terris* Institute, a trans-religious sanctuary in Warwick, NY, were outside the norm for most mystics, but they "seemed to be following in this tradition or else they could not have accomplished what they did. Day bridged the social justice divide within the religious and secular worlds and Franck did so within the world of artists and visionaries." Franck was a Zen Buddhist who became attracted to Catholicism due to the example of John XXIII. He assisted at the Vatican Council II where he used his artistic skills to draw all the sessions of the Council. Franck's artistic skills merged with his Zen experience in his *The Zen of Seeing*.
4 The pope's glocal revolution would have us examine how the Enlightenment overturned the "impregnable" intellectual, political, Christian edifice of the Middle Ages. The pope holds that to be evangelically enlightened, one must empty oneself in kenotic fashion. For us, this can include encountering the writings of Buddhist, Christian and Islamic mystics. The pope's awareness of the Christian

immanence-transcendence tradition can be complemented by the *sunyata* (Emptiness) views of Mahayana Buddhism "in which emptiness and fullness are dynamically identical." See *Paul Tillich and Asian Religions*, edited by Ka-fu Keith Chan, Yau-nang William Ng, (Berlin: de Gruyter, 2017), 64. As to total *Kenosis*, see Joe Lencioni, "Total *Kenosis*, True *Sunyata*, and the Plerotic Self of Thomas Merton and Masao Abe in *The Journal of Theta Alpha Kappa* Vol. 30, No. 1, Spring 2006.

5. In *A Brief History of Neoliberalism* (Oxford Univ. 2005), David Harvey argues that neoliberalism—the doctrine that market exchange is an "ethic" in itself, capable of acting as a guide for all human action—has become dominant in both thought and practice throughout much of the world since the 1970's. He analyzes the politico-economic dangers besetting us, and assesses the ethical alternatives being advocated by progressive movements.

6. Paul's mystical experience was not a purely intellectual exercise. It "brought about a complete change in his being and effected a life altering event for him." Barnabas Ahern, www.theway.org.uk/back/18Ahern.pdf

7. Antioch is where "Christian" was first applied to believers in Jesus—as opposed to Jews who did not so believe.

8. Joseph Grassi, *A World to Win: The Missionary Methods of Paul the Apostle*, (Orbis, 1965), 9.

9. Our neologism, "*glocally conscienticizing*," influenced by Paulo Freire, can be applied to the pope's writings.

10. Raymaker, *Third Way*, argues that mystics of all religions help lay the faith foundations that transcend beliefs.

11. Karen Armstrong, *Fields of Blood: Religion and the History of Violence*, 359, writes: "Like the weather, religion does lots of different things." To claim that it has a single, unchanging and inherently violent essence is not accurate. "Identical religious beliefs and practices have inspired diametrically opposed courses of action."

12. South East Asia's Theravada schools do not speak, as does Mahayana, of *sunyata* (emptiness) which in a way "parallels" Christian notions of *kenosis*. For some, Nagarjuna's view of emptiness is compatible with Theravada's Pali Canon according to which the Buddha never wanted us to become involved in any philosophical speculations. Theravada is not mystical. It holds that one must investigate oneself to understand fully the truth of suffering.

13 Pope Francis spoke of his mystical experience shortly before accepting his election as Bishop of Rome. When asked if he considered himself a mystic, the Pope replied that he rarely has had a mystical experience, but he did have one during the conclave shortly before his acceptance of his election as Pope. Before the acceptance, he asked to retire for some minutes in the next room. "My head was completely empty and a great anxiety invaded me," he said. "To make it pass and to relax, I closed my eyes and every thought disappeared, also that of refusing to accept the charge." Once he had closed his eyes, he felt no anxiety nor emotion, "but that at "a certain point a great light invaded me, it lasted for a second but it seemed really long." When the light dissipated he "headed to the room where the cardinals were waiting for me," and the table on which rested the act of acceptance. I signed it. https://www.catholicnewsagency.com/news/pope-experienced-a-great-light-before-accepting-the-papacy

14 Bob Roberts, Jr., *Transformation: How Glocal Churches Transform Lives and the World* (Zondervan, 2006).

15 Jean Houston, "Spirituality and the Meaning of Mysticism for Our Time."https://www.huffingtonpost.com/dr-jean-houston/spirituality-and-the-mean_b_620272.html See also http://www.jeanhouston.com/blog/?p=40

16 Jean Houston, http://enlightenedcatholicism-colkoch.blogspot.com/2010/09/mysticism-in-our-time.html In the stage of ecstasy, the Divine meets the mystic's psyche, which, cleared of the things that keep Reality at bay, ecstatically receives the One. That happiness, however, paradoxically leads to a "dark night of the soul."

17 Daniel Helminiak, *Brain, Consciousness, and God*. (State of New York, Univ. Press, 2015), 366. See also "Psychology goes 'glocal.' XXIX International Congress of Psychology on theme of 'Psychology and Globalization: Past, present, and future.' www.researchgate.net/publication/ 289730150_Psychology_goes_'glocal'_ Psychology's_adventure_in_Turkey. July, 2008. For Helminiak, theology tries to help us understand how God facilitates the very existence of our bodies and psyches through a theist faith able to discern broader horizons. As we do, he points to the intertwined nature of psychic problems which make conversion difficult to achieve.

18 *Laudato Si* (161) reads: "Doomsday predictions can no longer be met with irony or disdain. We may well be leaving to coming generations debris, desolation and filth. The pace of consumption, waste and

environmental change has so stretched the planet's capacity that our contemporary lifestyle (will) precipitate catastrophes."

19   https://cruxnow.com/analysis/2016/09/12/anniversary-can-finally-catch-benedicts-point-regensburg.

20   See http://w2.vatican.va/content/benedict-xvi/en/speeches/2005/august/documents/hf_ben-xvi_spe_ 20050820_meeting-muslims.html

21   Catherine Cornille, *The Im-Possibility of Interreligious Dialogue*, (Crossroad, 2008) argues that in the face of competing religious claims in our shrinking world, many turn to dialogue in hope of reducing violence. But all too often such dialogue fails due to not grasping the possibilities and limits of interreligious dialogue. One can best overcome the obstacles for dialogue through Conviction, Interconnection, Empathy, and Generosity.

22   The Coptic Church plays an important role in Christian-Islamic dialogue. A cardinal went to Cairo early in 2017 to initiate the formal dialogue process. Al Azhar and the Vatican now collaborate on important relevant issues.

23   "Grand Imam Calls on Middle East to 'Embrace' Christi https://insidethevatican.com/news/pope-meets-egypts-muslim-leader-ahmed-al-tayeb/ ans." Haaretz. February 5, 2019.

24   Pope Francis has transcended the papacy's usual boundaries. He has become a reconciling ambassador for peace. This was evident in his visits in 2017 to Myanmar and Bangladesh. Myanmar, a predominantly Buddhist country, has been accused of persecuting its Muslim minority population, the Rohingya people. Francis visited both countries even though Catholics make up only a tiny 1% of the populations of these two countries.

25   http://w2.vatican.va/content/francesco/en/speeches/2015/september/documents/papa-francesco_20150924_ usa-us-congress.html. The political theologian William Cavanaugh challenges the modern compartmentalization of religion and politics. Arguing that religious fervor never left — it has only migrated toward a new object of worship. His *Migrations of the Holy* (Grand Rapids, MI: Erdmans, 2011) examines the disconcerting modern transfer of sacred devotion from the church to the nation-state. He advocates a greater role for the church in post-secular public life. Critics of his genealogical and ecclesiological agenda argue that he has an illiberal understanding of politics and a triumphalist view of the church—one that Merton and Pope Francis have ecumenically avoided.

26 Patrick Hart, Jonathan Montaldo *The Intimate Merton: His Life from His Journals* (HarperOne, 2001).
27 Thomas Merton, *Conjectures of a Guilty Bystander* (New York: Doubleday, 1968) 85.
28 "Merton," *Catholic Sensibility*, https://catholicsensibility.wordpress.com/2006/09/20/115877968347365789/
29 Quoted in Michael Ford, *Masters for All Seasons* (Hidden Spring, 2009) 64.
30 Ichiro Okumura, *Awakening to Prayer*, Institute of Carmelite Studies, 1974. Hermann Cohen (1821–1871) was a noted German Jewish pianist, who converted to Catholicism. As a Discalced Carmelite priest, he was instrumental in re-establishing his Order in both France and England. In Kenya, the Carmelite priest, Onesmus Muthoka, converted from Protestantism to Catholicism www.ncronline.org/preview/carmelite-priest-useful-name-and-deed
31 Kirk Franklin, "Leading in Global-Glocal" (Ibid), See also Anton Geels, www.researchgate.net/publication/26889705_Glocal_spirituality_for_a_brave_new_world.
32 The need for a Christian glocal conscience is illustrated in a recent book that argues that indigenous and non-indigenous voices should partner in discussing both the wounds of colonial history and the opportunities for reconciliation between the church and indigenous peoples in Latin America. See Michel Andraos, *The Church and Indigenous Peoples in the Americas: In Between Reconciliation and Decolonization*, Eugene OR: Cascade Books, 2019. Many overlook the damage the Church caused to indigenous people during the colonial era. The Church's mission got entangled with the racist, opportunist colonialism found in the Doctrine of Discovery promoted by the infamous Pope Alexander VI on May 4, 1493, a year after Columbus' arrival in Hispaniolia. This "doctrine" supported Spain's strategy to ensure its exclusive right to the lands discovered by Columbus the previous year. Showing respect and admiration for indigenous people, Pope Francis upon his visit to Paraguay in July 2015, prayed the Lord's Prayer in Guaraní, the language of the country's indigenous people, spoken by 80% of the population. During a Mass in Ecuador in, 2015 Pope Francis included readings in Quichua, the most-spoken native language in Ecuador. He apologized to the indigenous peoples of the Americas for the "many grave sins" of colonial times and called for inviting indigenous people to be primary contributors to the dialogue whenever their land

is concerned. See https://blog.pachamama.org/pope-francis-changing-the-catholic-church-and-the-world

33 The Belgian Jesuit Dupuis' *Toward a Christian Theology of Religious Pluralism* (Orbis, 1997) led to his being investigated for unorthodoxy by the Vatican; he was vindicated in 2001.

34 For Bernard Lonergan, "Horizons," *Philosophical and Theological Papers 1965-1980*, 110, self-transcendence is "the possibility of horizon." Horizons differ from one another, from one subject to another, from one community to another, but a horizon should go beyond itself so as to give rise to other horizons. We seek horizons guided by the "possibility of willing what is truly good and doing it, of collaboration and true love, of swinging completely out of the habitat of an animal and of becoming a genuine person in human society." (Ibid). Only "a highly differentiated consciousness" can distinguish between the realms of meaning and effectively relate these realms to one another. Mere common sense procedures are unable to reach required self-transcendent standpoints for "dialoguing."

35 See William J. Wainwright, "Wilfred Cantwell Smith on faith and belief," *Religious Studies*, Sep. 1984. An eye of love is foundational faith. A Buddhist equivalent is recorded in Dogen's *Shobogenzo*: "bringing yourself to circumstances is delusional / recognizing yourself in circumstances is enlightenment." www.thezensite.com

36 See Bernard Lonergan, *Method in Theology*, 103, 119. Karen Armstrong acknowledges Smith and Lonergan as guiding luminaries in her own approach to compassion: https://charterforcompassion.org/karen-armstrong

37 See, for instance, David Henderson, "Carl Jung and Thomas Merton: Apophatic and Kataphatic Traditions in the 20th Century," *Studies in Spirituality*, 13/2003 (Leuven: Peeters, 263-91). Both men self-consciously addressed the dilemmas of modern man. "They reflected on Christianity, eastern religions, Native American spirituality, war, evil, symbolism, myth, consciousness, . . . but were conflicted about their power as leaders, teachers and public figures."

38 Hermann Häring, Janet Martin Soskice, Felix Wilfred, "Learning from other Faiths," *Concilium*, 2003, 141: "Medieval Jewish (as well as Muslim) philosophers identified belief in the Trinity with the heresy of *shituf* (Hebrew) or *shirk* (Arabic): 'associationism', or limiting the infinity of Allah by associating his divinity with creaturely being.

39 www.uua.org/offices/organizations/unitarian-universalist-mystics-

community. See also Raymaker, Grudzen, Holland, *Spiritual Paths to an Ethical & Ecological Global Civilization*. Pope Francis indicated that the document on Human Fraternity he signed with the Grand Imam of Al-Azhar, invites all persons who have faith in God and/or faith in human fraternity to unite and work together. http://w2.vatican.va/content/francesco/en/travels/2019/ outside/

40 Lonergan's notion of a transcultural theology with roots in the Old Testament (*Method in Theology*, 264) is equivalent to a glocal worldview. Both theologies recognize a transcultural base common to all human cultures.

41 Most human communication is "phatic," non-propositional; it "seeks to establish relationships rather than to convey ideas. A characteristic of autism (and the societal version of this malady) is characterized by isolationism- - a deficit in phatic communication. The world religions all have aspects of the apophatic (what is beyond words) and the kataphatic (what can be verbalized). See www.ignatianspirituality.com/2026/kataphatic-or-apophatic-prayer: "Kataphatic" prayer has content; it uses words, images, symbols, ideas. "Apophatic" prayer has no content. It means emptying the mind of words and ideas and simply resting in the presence of God.

42 Fetullah Gulen admits that the vast majority of Sufis have discouraged one from following the Sufi path without a *shaykh* or *pir*. Yet, a minority view holds that the spiritual guide need not be a living person. Kharaqani was initiated into the Sufi path by the spirit of Abu Yazid al-Bistami, while Attar was inspired by the spirit of Al-Hallaj. Other Sufis claimed to have as their guide Khidr, the mysterious companion of Moses whose story is recounted in the *Qur'an*. Gulen's position is that he is guided by the *Qur'an* and the Sunna: the *Qur'an* is not only the best guide, but is the source of all Sufi thought and practice. When this is supplemented by the views and experiences of later Sufis down through the centuries who applied the Qur'anic teachings through their own personal efforts (*ijtihad*), Sufism must *not* be considered an "alternative" path followed by some Muslims in contradistinction or in contradiction to the *sharia*; rather, Sufism should be regarded as one of the basic sciences of Islam.

43 William C. Chittick, "The Anthropology of Compassion," The Muhyiddin Ibn 'Arabi Society, Nov. 2009. Classical Sufi scholars define Tasawwuf as "a science whose objective is turning the heart away from all else but God. Sufism embodies the inner-esoteric dimension of Islam

which is complemented by outward or exoteric practices. Al-Ghazali, Rumi and other Sufis considered Sufism to be based upon the *Koran*. We view it as a dialogue partner.

44 The term secular society is tautological, because the ideal of secularity "is latent with the modern use of the term society.... Whatever comes after secularism ... won't be a 'society' any longer but rather another way for us to think about and give political form to the being-together of human beings." (Ibid). Remi Brague, "The Impossibility of Secular Society," www.firstthings.com/article/2013/10/the-impossibility-of-secular-society. Brague traces and faults the use of the term secularism by Holyoake (1817–1906) and to John Stuart Mill (1859).

45 Marianne Farina, CSC, *Sacred Conversations and the Evolution of Dialogue*,(New York: Paulist) 17. She relies on Lonergan's "transcendental method" that investigates how humans can be "attentive, intelligent, and responsible." See his *Method in Theology*, Herder, 1971,15. *Method* develops an eight-fold method for overall collaboration.

46 www.asianews.it/news-en/Pope:-at-this-troubled-time-in-history,-bishops-must-comfort,-help,-and-encourage-everyone,-without-distinction-34274.html on the pope's telling bishops that they must defend people's dignity.

47 "A vision underlies choice of Quevedo," *National Catholic Reporter*, Jan. 31-Feb. 13, 2014, 28. We speak of such a vision as that of "glocal Church," one that harmonizes the global and local. Romain Rolland won the 1915 Nobel Prize for literature due to his *Jean-Christophe* which depicts a harmony of opposites; an analogous harmony underlies the pope's glocal revolution which seeks to integrate the spiritual and material dimensions of life.

48 In the early Church, this vision was not one of a Universal Church, but one of a local self-governing churches. St. Irenaeus (130-202) did not attempt to refute the claims of the Gnostics on philosophical grounds but rather appealed to the written tradition found in the four Gospels. He lists the Bishops of Rome to show the unbroken succession from Peter to Eleutherius, the Bishop of Rome in that period. The Roman See had already assumed a preeminent place in the universal Church due to its exemplary community life and its central geographical position in the Roman empire. See R. A. Markus "Pleroma and Fulfilment: The Significance of History in St. Irenaeus' Opposition to Gnosticism" www.jstor.org/stable/1582753?seq=1#page_scan_tab_contents

49 "A vision underlies choice of Quevedo," *National Catholic Reporter*, Jan. 31-Feb. 13, 2014, 28.
50 www.spiegel.de/international/world/how-pope-francis-became-a-rebel-in-the-vatican-a-1035629.html
51 It is not easy to reform the Church. In diagnosing the recent divide within the Catholic Church, R. R. Reno. "The Populist Wave Hits the Catholic Church" (Nov. 13, 2018), speaks of a profound shift in the way a minority of U.S. Catholics who oppose Pope Francis portray him. Reno labels the Francis pontificate as "deregulatory," and in line with "a secular ruling establishment." See www.foreignaffairs.com/articles/world/2018-11-30/pope-francis-and-catholic-crisis. We stress that Francis is rethinking the Vatican's role in setting a new course for the Church today.
52 For us, Pope Francis is on the right side of history. Cardinal Raymond Burke, who strongly opposes the pope's reforms, alleges (*The Tablet, Catholic News Weekly*, April 7, 2018), that a pope's power is not "magical." If a pope deviates from the faith, he "must be disobeyed." The same forces that brought Trump and other rightists to power are leading the charge against Francis. The other side of the coin is that "much of the old imperial Catholicism may be crumbling. This is what is prodding a Steve Bannon to try to resuscitate it by erecting a curriculum for a right-wing Catholic institute in Italy. See Mark Hosenball, *The Tablet, Catholic News Weekly*, April 7, 2018.
53 Charles Taylor advocates a politics of difference and one of recognition to deal such problems of secularization and immigration. His *A Secular Age, Religion Today*, views today's sensibilities as subjectivist and instrumental. Joe Padilha, www.brainyquote.com/quotes/jose_padilha_490452 writes: "If you are in Brazil and you grew up in a right-wing dictatorship, you think Marxism is liberating. But if you grew up in Czechoslovakia, and the Soviet Union is controlling everything and killing people, then you think capitalism is liberating. Neither of those two things are true and it doesn't take a lot of brains to understand this." The challenge is to find a proper middle-way.
54 Referring to the great Buddhist scholar Nagarjuna's view that "emptiness" refers to the inter-functionality of all things, the Dalai Lama argues that this means we must respect nature. https://www.dalailama.com/ messages/ environment/buddhist-concept-of-nature. This view resonates with traditional and present Christian teachings.
55 When the Jesuits were gathered in the 36th General Congregation in

2016, Pope Francis addressed them on the topic "To Have Courage and Prophetic Audacity." He stressed 1) the need for courage and sincerity in one's testimony as rooted in the Christian tradition of opposing hypocrisy; 2) the famous maxim "to the greater glory of God." This implies "a living tension that reminds us how it is always possible to take a step forward from where we are, because our walk is in line with an ever more explicit manifestation of the glory of God. With the discernment of spirits we learn to recognize the good that dwells in each situation and to choose what leads to the greater good." See https://jesuits.org/Assets/Publications/File/GC36-Dialogue_of_Pope_Francis_ENGLISH.PDF

56 In pre-Industrial-Revolution days, international standards did not exist. It did not matter that there were non-uniform local times in each town and station. The development of railroads required a standard time for all. While uniform standards are needed across the technological spectrum, democratic standards can be undermined—a poisonous development. This fact illustrates quite well what glocal means today. Locally, governments can pass anti-democratic laws, but globally this leads to the problems now confronting "open borders."

57 R. Mickens. https://international.la-croix.com /news/ the-roman-catholic-church-continues-to-implode/5616 On "The radical theological vision of Pope Francis" and his renewed theology for our turbulent times, R. Mickens https://international.la-croix.com/news/the-radical-theological-vision-of-pope-francis/10477, Mickens adds: "Since the early days of his pontificate Francis has shown himself to be non-ideological and surprisingly non-partisan. Despite the ranting of some of his detractors, even within the most intransigent sectors of the Church's hierarchy, this pope is very definitely Catholic. But even more than that he is a Christian."

58 By establishing a new "super-dicastery" with his Apostolic Constitution *Praedicate evangelium* ("Preach the Gospel"), Pope Francis has cemented his revolution of making the Good News the very center of the Church's life. This complements his other revolution of conscientizing humans as to the socio-political realities of oppression in ways that can circumvent those who are trying to subvert his policies by appealing to those of Benedict XVI.

CHAPTER 5

Pope Francis's Glocal Engagements with the Middle East and Africa

Globalization is not only an economic phenomenon; it has had important religious-cultural dimensions that have exacerbated today's sectarian violence. In trying to find the balance between one's sense of identity and surviving in a glocalized world, one should not ignore the religious dimension as does Thomas Friedman in his *The World is Flat*.[1] The Middle East has been the source of many of the religious conflicts among Jews, Christians and Muslims. The three "religions of the Book" all claim Abraham as father of their beliefs. Although the conflicts are motivated by politics, religion has played important roles both in uniting the people of the Middle East and in dividing them. To better understand present problems and to formulate strategies for bridging the divides, we shall briefly examine some historical contexts. In his outreach to moderate Islamic nations, Pope Francis is sharing faith-hope-love links that might help lessen conflicts and lead to hopeful solutions. In some respects, the birth of glocal societies began in the Middle Ages when Jews, Christians and Muslims created a scientific-technological culture that led to the formation of Western universities (12th to 13th centuries). Pope Urban II's call for the First Crusade (1095) is still a source of Christian-Islamic quarrels. Although the crusades ended in failure, it is often overlooked that after plundering Palestine, the Crusaders brought back many spiritual-medical-philosophical resources that helped transform the West. Humbly acknowledging the West's debt to Islam could help blunt the increasingly sectarian nature of Christian-Muslim encounters. Muslims' deep resentment of the Crusades has led them to refer to the western invaders of Afghanistan and Iraq as modern day "Crusaders." Colonization, the result of Western technological prowess, in turn led migrations from former colonies and much distrust between Muslims and Europeans.[2] If globalization is an irreversible phenomenon with its attendant religious dimensions, we are now faced with the urgent need to learn from history so as to help guide the future. The Church seems particularly well poised to help the West and the wider world understand relevant implications with a view to heal.

Some Historical Lessons to Help "Guide" the Future

In the first period of globalization (lasting from the Middle Ages through the Renaissance),[3] scholars from the monotheistic faith traditions provided a scientific-technological basis for a global economic transformation that eventually led to the Industrial Age in the 17th and 18th centuries. This initial period included the transfer of scientific and technical knowledge from the Islamic civilization of the Middle East and North Africa to the Christian West. It also led to the West's intellectual revival through its new model of university-based scientific and philosophical education. It saw the voyages of discovery that used the developing scientific discoveries in navigation and weaponry that would enable the West to colonize and exploit the natives of Africa and the Americas from 1500 to 1900—through the African slave trade and the destruction of native cultures in the Americas by Spanish, English and other European colonialists. Further explorations into Asian and South Asia led to the colonization of India, Indochina and various parts of Africa by European nations. The Church was complicit in extending Spanish and Portuguese domination of native populations in Africa, South and Central America and the Philippines.

During the Arab Spring, which began in Tunisia in 2010, and then spread to other countries in the Middle East and North Africa in 2011, there was hope that democracy might take root there. Instead, most of these countries have been taken over by authoritarian regimes that crush dissent. The youth under these regimes have mostly lost hope in the political process. Some have turned to radical ideologies and the violence of such groups as Al Qaeda, ISIS, Boko Haram and Al-Shabab. There have been frequent terrorist attacks that have attempted to destabilize North Africa (Egypt, Libya and Tunisia), Central Africa (Mali, Nigeria) and East Africa (Somalia and Kenya). Pope Francis has sought to align the Church with tolerant Muslim organizations and Muslim majority countries that promote peaceful solutions for the problems facing this increasingly perilous area of the globe.

Pope Francis Implementing Christian-Muslim Lessons Learned during the Middle Ages

Because of the contacts between Islamic and Christian philosophers and scientists in the Middle Ages, Richard Bulliet makes a case for a single historical Islamic-Christian Civilization.[4] His conciliatory approach to

Islamic culture stands in sharp contrast to Samuel Huntington's view on the "Clash of Civilizations." Huntington argues that people's cultural and religious differences have been the primary source of conflict in the post-Cold War world. He claims that this is likely to continue on the model of the fall of the Shah of Iran—followed by the detention of American diplomatic personnel in Tehran in 1979—and the terrorist attacks of September 11, 2001.[5] Despite recent setbacks, Bulliet argues that, as in the past, dramatic events can catalyze changes. He recalls the common heritage of Christianity and Islam in the cultures of the Middle East, North Africa and Spain. A fundamental restructuring of Western thinking about relations with Islam calls for a fresh look at the historical development of Western Christendom and Islam. These two parallel one another so closely that the two entities can best be thought of as two versions of common socio-religious systems—including the respective divisions between Orthodox and Western forms of Christianity and Sunni-Shiites divisions. In both cases there are different versions of one socio-religious system. For eight centuries, the pathways of development led in the same direction. Occasionally these pathways virtually overlapped one another. (Bulliet, 9).

It is important to note that Pope Francis has the needed glocal eye of love to focus on the positive side of problems haunting humanity. His ability to transcend local divisions is nurtured by his focus on the positive side of conflicts. He suggests incremental steps toward solutions. Our discussion of a glocal, ethical spirituality is premised on the common prophetic heritage of the three monotheistic religions as crucial to mediating between developing nations and Westerners willing to help them. By establishing common faith-ethical frameworks rooted in these three religions and those of eastern spiritualities such as the Buddhist ethic of compassion, religious leaders could forge a common alliance with political and business associates to address the global economic and educational imbalances now exacerbating the divide between rich and poor nations (and similar imbalances *within* national boundaries).

In February, 2019, Pope Francis made the first papal visit to the United Arab Emirates (UAE), one of the few Muslim majority countries to allow its large Christian minority population to publicly practice its faith. This was a landmark trip for it was the first-ever papal visit to the Arabian Peninsula, the birthplace of Islam. Pope Francis used the occasion to call for an end to the violence in Yemen which has brought about an ever-worsening humanitarian crisis. Francis' public mass in the capital city of Abu Dhabi drew about 4,000 Muslims among the 135,000 people present. Many of the attendees were Catholic migrants from places such as the Philippines and South America.⁶ In conjunction with Pope Francis' visit to the UAE, the Global Conference on Human Fraternity in Abu Dhabi,⁷ there took place a meeting with 700 representatives from the world's religions. It was the first of its kind in the Arab world. Clerics and scholars in attendance represented the Muslim, Jewish, Hindu, Sikh, Buddhist and other faiths from throughout the world. In his address to this group, the pope said:

> The enemy of fraternity is an individualism which translates into the desire to affirm oneself and one's own group above others. This danger threatens all aspects of life, even the highest innate prerogative of man, that is, the openness to the transcendent and to religious piety. True religious piety consists in loving God with all one's heart and one's neighbor as oneself. Religious behavior ... needs continually to be purified from the recurrent temptation to judge others as enemies and adversaries. Each belief system is called to overcome the divide between friends and enemies, in order to take up the perspective of heaven, which embraces persons without ... discrimination.⁸

Pope Francis has become a leader in promoting greater understanding and toleration of religious and cultural diversity in both the Middle East and Africa. In 2016, he met with Hasan Rouhani, the president of Iran. This encounter at the Vatican opened new opportunities for dialogue about the ongoing political and military conflicts in the Middle East. The two leaders stressed "the importance of interreligious dialogue in promoting reconciliation and peace."⁹ The Holy See may play a role in acting as a neutral mediator among the Sunni and Shia states in the Middle East. In his World Day of Peace, 2017, message on non-violence, Francis emphasized the constructive role that non-violence can play in world affairs. It presents the best hope¹⁰ for a solution to the epidemic of violence plaguing humanity.

A Potential for Conversions in Africa— with Some Inbuilt Problems

As of 2018 Africa replaced Latin America as the continent with the largest Christian population.¹¹ It now has approximately 630 million Christians versus 600 million in Latin America.¹² It continues to position itself as the future axis of Catholicism, with the number of baptized Catholics on the continent growing at a significantly faster rate than anywhere else in the world. According to the numbers released the Vatican, Catholicism grew globally from 1.272 billion in 2014 to 1.285 in 2015. This represents a 1% annual growth, and 17.7% of the world's population. Growth varies radically from one continent to another. While in Africa the Catholic population grew by 19.4%, it has remained stable in Europe. If anything, it is decreasing on the so-called "Old Continent," where the birth rate is low and population is projected to decrease in upcoming years, with more people dying than being born in several countries.[13]

Some of the first Christian churches began in Egypt. The first Christian theological center was located in Alexandria. Today the growth of the Church in Africa today is largely occurring in sub-Saharan regions. The world's largest Catholic seminary is in Nigeria. Nairobi hosts 11 major seminaries and several facilities to train nuns and laity. The growth of the Catholic Church in Africa is both a blessing and a challenge since it has only limited educational and social resources to develop its rapidly growing communities. Despite such limitations, many African priests now work in various parts of the world. Africa has become one of the centers for the recruitment and training of priests. As to overall growth demographics, the NGO Population Reference Bureau foresees that some West African countries could see their population grow more than 2.5 times by 2050. Cédric Mayrargue, a French expert on Africa, notes that the continent still has lots of potential for conversions. "Whole areas still practice traditional religions and are considered mission territories. This is reflected in the percentage of baptisms received after the age of seven (33%) almost twice as high as the world average."[14] For Philippe Hugon, another French expert on Africa, there is also a social component to the phenomenon: "In Africa, the priest not only has a religious role but also a status, close to that of a teacher, as in Europe in the 19th century." Being ordained opens the door to a "certain renown that attracts many young people."[15]

Clearly, Christianity is experiencing a New Pentecost in Africa. Christianity cannot survive in a healthy state unless it be a force for transformation in a globalized and secularized world. In a book on African theology and spirituality, the Jesuit A. E. Orobator[16] writes that before his conversion to Christianity, he was raised in the practice of animism, the traditional African religion. This repository of African religion, he maintains is at its heart "a deep belief in the livingness of creation." It is the soil in which both Christianity and Islam have taken root. Orobator examines the living interplay between African Religion, Christianity, and Islam in Africa. He argues that the religious experience and the spiritual imagination of Africa combine to offer a wisdom capable of renewing the global community of believers. Among these gifts are a deep consciousness of transcendence in day-to-day living; reverence towards human and natural ecologies; and a holistic understanding of creation and shared responsibility of stewardship for the universe. With Orobator, we are suggesting along with many other theologians, that, as was the case with the early Church, the Church must once again focus on relevant forms of communal experiences such as we also find, for example, in China where Christianity has become to a large extent a home-based movement.

Africa faces many challenges such as the realities of evolving gender roles and the need for sophisticated forms of education. Lay people must be trained to serve in such diverse ministries as interreligious dialogue, youth ministries, social inequality, and environmental challenges. It is with this aim in mind, that the Jesuits established in Nairobi the Hekima Institute for Peace Studies and International Relations. In addition to the dialogue with Islam, the Catholic Church in Africa is faced with the challenge of the spread of Pentecostal churches. The latter have "advantages" the Catholic Church lacks: they offer an easy path to become an ordained minister, and they allow a married clergy—which resonates with African culture. Further, the growth of the Prosperity Gospel in Africa has been propelled through the use of new technologies effectively used to promote its ministries. Just as the proliferating Mega-Churches in the US and in Latin America have drawn Catholics into their communities, a similar pattern has begun to emerge in Africa. Many of these churches can rely on sister congregations in the U.S. to help them grow their flocks. The African Catholic Church should learn to partner with more affluent Catholic congregations in the US to support its ministerial needs and to improve the training of priests as well as of religious and lay ministers.

Anticipating Future Developments in the Global Church

The decline of the Church in Europe came about because it failed to adapt to the changing nature of society. Part of Pope Francis' vision is to give each region of the Church the ability to discern new strategies and plans for evangelization[17] and mission. Africa is becoming more urbanized—causing many changes in social and cultural patterns. Most Africans can access cell phones. Many use What's App to connect with friends and colleagues. Due to this, the African churches need more expertise in popular technologies. The growth of such technologies will require the Church to venture into the social media that has been used effectively by Jihadist groups to attract youth to their extremist ideology. Africa has increasingly been an area of concern due to recruitment of youth for Al Qaeda and ISIS-affiliated groups. East Africa has been at the center of the struggle for the "hearts and minds" of Muslim youth. The perception among many Muslim youths is that the Kenyan government is aligned with the U. S. in fighting Al-Shabab. Unemployment among Muslim youth in Kenya is high—up to 75%.[18] As a result, Al-Shabab attacks on Christian communities have become common in the coastal region of Kenya.

Africa is a very young continent, development-wise. The future of the Church, of course, depends upon its youth. Both in Africa and in the West, the Church must focus on effective mission strategies that appeal to the young. We shall examine, in Chapter 8, the role of the Small Christian Communities, asking how such communities can help youth actively participate in the Church's overall mission. Here, we stress that the social justice ministries of the Church in Africa have an important role to play in this respect. In his visit to Kenya in 2015, Pope Francis met with governmental leaders in Nairobi—including President, Uhuru Kenyatta—and members of the clergy. He visited a Nairobi slum where a Jesuit parish is located. He also met with thousands of Kenyan youth at a sports stadium. Speaking about the dangers of tribalism and fanaticism that betray our common humanity, he stressed the need for youth to dialogue. He asked them to hold each other's hands as a sign of offsetting the tribalism plaguing Kenya.[19]

Some Noteworthy Projects That Concretely Address the Christian-Muslim Divides in Kenya

One of the key Catholic leaders in the interfaith movement in Kenya has been Father Wilybard Lagho, Vicar General of the Archdiocese of Mombasa, a former Chairperson of the Coast Interfaith Council of Clerics (CICC). In 2012, Lagho asked Gerry and Marita Grudzen to visit with himself and Bishop Lele of Mombasa the Lamu Archipelago with a view to expand the work of CICC to include Interfaith training for religious and lay leaders in the coastal region. With the assistance of the Louvain Alumni Association of the US, the Grudzens were able to fund the initiation of annual interfaith leadership training programs in the coastal region of Kenya. This program, known as "Paths to Peace Kenya,"[20] has joined others in trying to improve interfaith relations in Kenya's coastal region. Its peace-and-justice initiative educates

Kenyan youth. Some graduates of this initiative have developed an interfaith cultural program for the children of the Lamu bordering Somalia. This is the area that was attacked by Al-Shabab in 2014. In 2015, six teachers, three Christian and three Muslim—all affected by the Al-Shabab attacks—were invited to share in Paths to Peace's week-long interfaith seminar at Nairobi's Maryknoll Center. With help from Columbia Univ., Nairobi, and the Muslim Respect Foundation, the Grudzens conducted a week-long seminar.

Over the next two years, Christian and Muslim teachers in Lamu, led by graduates of the Paths to Peace program, created an interfaith cultural program in music, poetry and drama. The program has helped reduce the fear that had prevented many Christian youths from going to school for several months after the Al-Shabab attacks. As a result, the teachers who came from the affected Lamu region agreed to take part in a multi-year cultural project with the teachers and students in their region so as to help allay remaining fears due to the Al-Shabab attacks. In 2017, the teachers, students and administrators from the Lamu region along with the Grudzens further developed the program. The ongoing program testifies to the importance of education in dealing with the fear and prejudice caused by terrorist acts. In their 2018 meetings, the concerned leaders from Lamu Island and Mombasa expressed their glocal solidarity as they developed further interfaith training programs. In 2018, the Grudzens again partnered with the Hekima Institute to develop a curriculum that will complement the ongoing interfaith curriculum of the previous five years. They believe that engaging in prophetic dialogue should be part of the Africa's mission. During his 2015 visit to Nairobi, Pope Francis emphasized the need to confront the problem of tribalism on the African continent. He called on the youth of Kenya to overcome the tribal divisions that have led to strife and violence around an electoral process. The effects of colonialism are still being felt in many parts of Africa. Africa has many natural resources such as oil and minerals. Because of the lack of technical expertise, it will be difficult for countries such as Kenya to find the best arrangements for use of their natural resources. The more developed countries of the world will attempt to exploit these for their own advantage. Kenya has entered into various agreements with China to develop both its port facilities near Lamu Island and its internal rail infrastructure. The Jesuit Institute of Peace Studies is helping leaders evaluate Kenya's contracts with foreign governments. The Church would do well to exercise its prophetic role in developing nations. It must take an active role in training all segments of society to participate in such negotiations among governments. Relevant to this challenge is Bernard-Henri Levy's book, *The Empire and the Five Kings*, which argues that the five "Kings" (China, Iran, Turkey, Russia and Sunni Radical Islam) are vying to set the agenda for the world. Each of them is pursuing its own cause, its own interests which are often at variance with Africa's best interests. Africa needs the type of long-term vision that Pope Francis has for the common good of humanity; it will be at the center of the Church's mission for the foreseeable future. We may even see an African pope by the end of the present century.

Notes

1. Thomas Friedman, *The World Is Flat: A Brief History of the Twenty-first Century* (Farrar, Straus and Giroux, 2005).
2. The rise of right-wing parties in the West opposing immigration bring issues of cultural integration into focus.
3. Walter Ong, *The Presence of the Word: Some Prolegomena for Cultural and Religious History* (New Haven: Yale Press) 1967, 112, 314, points out that throughout the Middle Ages "visualism" was important but was raised to a new prominent intensity with the invention of alphabetic topography. This then led to a reconditioning of human consciousness by media that accentuate sound. Ong sought to help humans today understand the anthropological functions of feelings and valuing so that men and women might newly experience the depths of their souls.
4. Richard W. Bulliet, *The Case for Islamo-Christian Civilization* (NY: Columbia University Press, 2004), 7.
5. Samuel Huntington, *The Clash of Civilization: Remaking of the World Order* (Simon and Schuster, 1996). Such tragedies had been preceded by such events as the fall of Crusader Jerusalem to Saladin in 1187, the loss of Byzantine Constantinople to the Ottomans in 1453, and the nearly successful Ottoman siege of Vienna in 1529.
6. *Vox*. Feb 5, 2019. https://www.vox.com/2019/2/5/18211956/pope-francis-mass-united-arab-emirates-arab
7. In contrast to these positive developments, compare the extremely complicated situations of ISIS terrorism in the desert between Eastern Syria and Western Iraq or the history of Khalifa Haftar in Libya: www.alaraby.co.uk/ english/indepth/2019/4/10/who-is-khalifa-haftar-libyas-cia-linked-rogue-general-turned-warlord
8. "Pope in UAE: Address to Fraternity Conference," www.vaticannews.va/en/pope/news/2019-02/pope-francis-uae-global-conference-

human-fraternity-full-text.html To grasp the importance of the UAE message, recall that Silsilah (Arabic: سلسلة) is an Arabic word meaning chain, link, connection often used in various senses of lineage such as when a Sufi master transfers his *khilfat* (spiritual authority) to his spiritual descendant. It is in this sense that in Mindanao in the Philippines, an island long beset with Christian-Islamic conflicts, greeted the UAE message as a sign of hope providing a sound basis for its own Silsilah Islamic-Christian "glocally inspired" type of dialogue.

9   https://www.nytimes.com/2016/01/27/world/middleeast/pope-francis-hassan-rouhani-meeting.html   In a way, Francis was doing what St. Francis did in 1218 when he visited the sultan in Egypt on a mission of peace.

10 https://w2.vatican.va/content/francesco/en/messages/peace/documents/papa-francesco_20161208_messaggio-l-giornata-mondiale-pace-2017.html Samuel Johnson also stressed that "Hope is necessary in every condition. The miseries of poverty, sickness and captivity would, without this comfort, be insupportable."

11 Fr. Alain Clément Amiéz, *Baptism and prophetic commitment for an adult Church in Africa*, argues that Africa is producing baptized people, not Christians. He asks for an adult Church in Africa. *La Croix Africa*, Jan. 9, 2019.

12 https://aleteia.org/2018/07/24/africa-overtakes-latin-america-for-the-highest-christian-population/

13 "Vatican statistics confirm the Catholic future is in Africa," *Crux*. April 6, 2017. https://cruxnow.com/global-church/2017/04/06/vatican-statistics-confirm-catholic-future-africa/

14 https://international.la-croix.com/news/the-evolution-of-catholicism-in-africa/5210

15 https://international.la-croix.com/news/the-evolution-of-catholicism-in-africa/5210 May 20, 2017.

16 A. E. Orobator, *Religion and Faith in African: Confessions of an Animist* (Orbis: 2018.) The book is based on the prestigious Duffy Lectures he delivered at Boston College.

17 On June 21, 2019, Pope Francis in a talk in Naples reminded us that contemplation and presentation of the heart is at the core of the Church's kerygma. This core along with dialogue should be the criteria for renewing studies. It "means that they are at the service of the path of a Church that increasingly puts evangelization at the center. Not apologetics, not manuals, as we heard, but evangelizing. At the

center is evangelizing, which is not the same thing as proselytizing. In dialogue with cultures and religions, the Church announces the Good News of Jesus and the practice of evangelical love which He preached as a synthesis of the whole teaching of the Law, the message of the Prophets and the will of the Father. Dialogue is above all a method of discernment and proclamation of the Word of love which is addressed to each person and which wants to take up residence in the heart of each person. Only in listening to this Word and in the experience of love that it communicates can one discern the relevance of kerygma." http://w2.vatican.va/content/francesco/en/speeches/2019/june/documents/papa-francesco_2021621_teologia-napoli.html

18 Gerald Grudzen, *Burying the Sword: Confronting Jihadism with Interfaith Education.* Author House. 2017, 48-49.
19 Pope Francis Youth Assembly in Kenya, November 27, 2015. https://www.youtube.com/watch?v=VqotRRUQBR0 He told Christian and Muslim religious leaders that they have little choice but to engage in dialogue to guard against the "barbarous" extremist attacks that have struck Kenya: religious leaders must be "prophets of peace" in a world sown by hatred. He said interfaith dialogue isn't a luxury or optional—it is simply and clearly "essential."
20 See https://www.facebook.com/pathstopeacekenya/ In 2012, Global Ministries University established a peace education program for Christian and Muslim teachers working in the coastal region of Kenya. This foreshadowed Pope Francis' suggestion on the need for peaceful collaboration between Christians and Muslims.

CHAPTER 6
The Church in Latin America

It is not only Africa that needs a long-term vision of the type Pope Francis advocates for glocal churches. Part 3 will explore how some Catholics on all continents have pioneered glocal, evangelical ways to partly offset the evils of capitalism by way of liberation theologies and small Christian Communities.[1] This chapter examines the tragic effects caused by neo-liberalism in many parts of Latin America. It argues that types of community-based life practiced by indigenous populations are part of the solution.[2]

Problems Caused by Neo-Liberalist Ideologies in Many Parts of Latin America

In March, 2019, speaking to a group of young Latin Americans on the Church's social doctrine, Pope Francis said that "Engaging in politics inspired by the Gospel (is)...a powerful way to clean up our fragile democracies."[3] As priest and bishop in Argentina, Francis had to deal with neo-liberalist, fascist governments. His relationship with the Mafia-connected, now President, Mauricio Macri of Argentina was one of mutual distrust. Macri has spent his career in anti-immigrant, corporation-oriented politics.[4] Successive governments in Argentina have favored large agro-industry, petroleum, telecommunication, electricity, water, and banking conglomerates (*grupos económicos*) who pressure the government to compensate them "for their losses due to capital flight, etc."[5] The conglomerates have long reigned supreme while being contested by some popular, civil organizations. In Argentina, as in many other Latin American countries, neoliberalism and fascism have long intermeshed. Archbishop Romero was killed for opposing such a system in El Salvador. In Brazil, Notre Dame de Namur sister Dorothy Stang was murdered in 2005 in Anapu, a city in the state of Pará, at the hands of a rancher due to her efforts to help the landless. She had chosen to live in extreme poverty in order to help others living in poverty. She had a passion for people of all cultures, for social justice, peacemaking, fairness, and respect for the environment. She possessed few material things: a mix-match of colorful clothing, spartan furnishings and her Bible, which she carried everywhere. Sometimes she called it her "weapon." Thirteen years after her murder, there developed a surreal scenario in which a President Bolsonaro supporter worked to imprison Sister Stang's successor, Father José Amaro Lopes de Souza, falsely accusing him of extortion when, in fact, he was an unrelenting defender of human rights—as local bishops have testified.[6] What is important to note in this surreal scenario is that it incarnates evil. One recalls the fascist mentality of Stroessner in Paraguay and Pinochet in Chile that assumed the legitimacy of neocolonialist ideology. It embodies the evils Pope Francis has been exposing—being the very opposite of glocal-ethical concerns, of any authentic religious foundations. It completely and cold-bloodedly[7] subverts community values and the common good with its neoliberalist illusions of uncontrolled market dominance.

Socialist-Neoliberalist Confrontation in Chile: How Pinochet Subverted Authentic Values

Another example of how neoliberalism became dominant in Latin America is found in Chile. In 1970, Salvador Allende was elected president of Chile. Earlier, when he was Minister of Health, Allende had published a book that argued that the poor lack sufficient incomes to clothe and feed their families, that workers lack protection against harsh climate and employment conditions. As president, he promoted socialist economic reforms which helped awaken citizens and organize to support socialist programs. He saw to it that assemblies of workers were formed in factories. Owners alleged that this was modelled on the way the Russian soviets had launched the revolutions of 1905 and 1917. The Chilean councils—*"cordones"* in Spanish—began making decisions about conditions of life and work across the country. In September 1973, the Army Chief of Staff, Augusto Pinochet took over the government. The military used the alleged breakdown of democracy and the economic crisis that took place during Allende's presidency to justify its seizure of power. Pinochet was later indicted and charged with a number of crimes but was never convicted.[8] He died in 2006. It may be well to contextualize such happenings in Latin America by reaching further back into history and the cultural heritage of Latin America.

Appreciating the Wealth and Beauty of the Andean Cultural Heritage

Steve P. Judd has written about the indigenous theology movement in Latin America, emphasizing that there is "hope at the crossroads" at the point "where two distinct worlds meet"[9] in a *"Teologia India."* Judd goes into "the emerging paradigms for intercultural dialogue, where different cultures share the richness and wisdom of their respective ancestral heritage, the gift they are to each other—above and beyond whatever material wealth might ordinarily separate them." (Ibid 211). Reaching back into history, Judd refers to *apacheta*, piles of stones left by travelers on high mountain passes as offerings.

Judd argues that *apachetas* "mark the turning points in the journeys of a people to greater self-understanding and awareness of their place in history according to cyclical patterns." (Ibid). This is in contrast to Western *linear* visions of history. "Yet at this real or imaginary crossroads they enter into relationships with the 'other' who is different." (Ibid). It makes it possible for indigenous people to recover their identity and to affirm a place of respect in the worldwide Christian movement. Latin America's erstwhile "invisible people" have now become visible actors on the world stage—thanks to the influence of Vatican II and Medellin Bishops' Conference of 1968. The Latin American Church has had to distance itself from being identified with powerful elites as it implements its option for the poor.

Judd stresses the importance of honoring the religious worldview of indigenous people within broader social movements. This implies, for example, recovering the tradition of figures like the 16th century Dominican missionary Bartolome de Las Casas (1484-1566) who emphasized a "prophetic and peaceful evangelization based on the encounter with the "other." This, in turn, "had inspired others like the Jesuits in their utopian social projects and experiments of the Reduction that prospered in the 17th and 18th centuries in the areas of what are now eastern Bolivia, Paraguay, Brazil, and Argentina." (Ibid, 213).

In reality, there have been some painful moments in the march toward recognizing the rights and traditions of indigenous peoples in South America. Judd recalls, for example, that when Pope John II visited Cusco, Peru in 1985, "an indigenous religious leader boldly thrust a Bible into the pope's hands as a sign of returning the Bible, saying that indigenous peoples were never consulted whether they wanted the Bible in the first place."[10] Judd adds that this awkward incident did alert the Vatican toward more fully appreciating indigenous culture. This led to an "out-of-the-cave-and-into-the-limelight" theological process and the creation of "networks for continuous interchange across the continent." (Ibid, 217-18). From our glocal standpoint of focusing on Pope Francis' ministry,[11] the theological networks Judd refers to are instances of efforts to integrate globalization processes within local traditions. In preparation for the 1997 Synod for the Americas, Judd had written that a consensus had been reached that it was an "opportune occasion to reflect on a shared history of solidarity and collaboration as well as an often stormy relationship marked by conflict and suspicion. No sector within the North American church should welcome this development more than the U.S. missionary movement - past, present and future. It was from the perspective of this movement,[12] that Judd was addressing the challenges of that Synod. We shall apply this perspective to integrate the roles of Christian communities and their transformations.

Glocally Integrating the Ideals of a Viable Global Community Adapted to Local Needs

With respect to liberation theology and praxis, Gustavo Gutiérrez stresses that liberation theology is "a critical reflection on Christian praxis in light of the word of God.'"[13] Rather than viewing culture normatively, it draws on the concrete experience and situation of a local people. It focuses on the huge disparity between rich and poor, on the roles of the military and on uneven economic development. Liberation theology does raise questions about the very nature of Christianity and of theology; therefore, its implications extend beyond the boundaries of South America to the whole Church. In *A Theology of Liberation*, Gutiérrez defines theology as a critical reflection on a praxis committed to take actions in the social political sphere in light of the Gospel. He writes of the growing awareness of humankind as an active subject of history, ever more articulate in the face of social injustice and human trauma.[14] Liberation theology identifies with and is in solidarity with the poor. It inverts the traditional view of orthodoxy leading to orthopraxis. It seeks to transform the world in the light of the Gospel, and it is the experience of this action and struggle which leads to a better knowledge of God, to orthodoxy. Theology therefore is a reflection on pastoral activity. This in turn informs future pastoral activity. Making use of theories from the social sciences, "Gutiérrez opposes developmentalism, which time and time again has failed, and proposes liberation—a radical new social and economic system to counter poverty and oppression. While envisioning a new social order or utopia, he cautions that every such attempt must be judged by the "eschatological proviso" that the Kingdom is yet to come.[15]

Applying Lonergan's Glocal Notion of Cosmopolis to God-Centered Liberation Movements

Lonergan speaks of a cultural community or "*cosmopolis*" that transcends the frontiers of states and the epochs of history. Cosmopolis is not an unrealized political ideal but "a longstanding, nonpolitical, cultural fact,"[16] (we name it a glocal notion of *cosmopolis*) that avoids totalizing views. Such an ideal cultural community can help us adjust theology's radical breakthroughs to Pope Francis' ministry. It embraces the particularity of one's own cultural, religious, and intellectual traditions, while remaining radically open to dialogue with the other. By doing so, education for cosmopolis fosters both authentic appropriation and reflective critique of one's own traditions, as well as an appreciation for the authenticity of others. . .. (It) is an invitation to dialogue which promotes mutual understanding, mutual respect, and mutual interdependence in a globalized world.[17]

We are concerned about implementing authentic values glocally. From a Christian point of view, Jesus' teaching on the Kingdom in the synoptic gospels is authentic, having a sense of radical inclusion about it. It calls for transformative change when sinners are "called to repentance" (Luke 5:32). Jesus' kingdom is contrasted with the "ruler of this world" (John 12:13) who is overthrown by the triumphant sacrifice of Jesus on the cross. This cosmic contrast is continued in St. Paul for whom the Kingdom separates those who are "'in Christ' and those who are not" (1 Cor 6:11). Lonergan's vision of a glocal cosmopolis calls us to be attentive, intelligent, reasonable, and responsible in all aspects of life. As alienation and ideology destroy community, "so self-sacrificing, Christian love reconciles alienated man to his true being, and undoes the mischief initiated by alienation and consolidated by ideology."[18] Our hope is that people today might live Kingdom values in a world intent on self-serving power politics. Long gone are the days when politics was conducted in benign face-to-face relationships. We now live in a quasi-nihilist culture influenced by fake news and by cynical Machiavellian politics. Still, an authentic glocal cosmopolis, fostering the Kingdom of God, calls us to live self-transcending values for the benefit of all.[19] Liberation theologians in Latin America and Lonergan's notion of cosmopolis as cultural community have made the necessary value judgments to help free the oppressed from dehumanizing conditions.

Conclusion to Chapter Six

Community life has played a central role in Pope Francis' ministry. It is also a central aspect of how indigenous people have lived across the globe. One serves God and neighbor through responsible community living. Our examination of various situations in Latin America has stressed the need for people to truly encounter one another as a preamble to forming authentic communities. This requirement applies to authentic, glocal community life anywhere. Thus we can ask "How share the depth of one's inner self with others so as to build better, viable communities? How may we empower one another?" The various facets of our "inner and outer lives" call for a realistic optimism.[20] Christian life has often been lived in flawed ways as is evident in the dualist tendencies of Western thought. As a corrective to dualism, we have appealed to Jesus' holistic vision and to indigenous notions of solidarity. We have suggested that the West can learn much from such solidarity. People across the planet depend on one another socially, economically and politically. It is indispensable to discern persons' inner lives[21] and to relate this to glocal, communal forms of spirituality. Many today downplay religion, but they cannot explain away the sense of mystery pervading our lives. Since his early days of his ministry in Argentina, Pope Francis has stressed that living the Good News of Jesus should be our key priority.

The following chapter on compassionate ways of healing in Asia and on the repressive measures of Communist regimes illustrate the polar opposites of being open to a glocal faith or of being driven by ideologies that tolerate little or no dissent. The irony is that only by being glocally open to a genuine spirituality could ideological regimes remedy and be freed from their intolerant, self-serving agenda.

Notes

1 For Joseph Healey and Jeanne Hinton, *Small Christian Communities Today* (Orbis, 2005), churches everywhere can learn from thriving small Christian communities. They advocate what we call glocal ways of being Church.

2 On the Mayan indigenous theology movement in Chiapas, Mexico in which young people are rediscovering their identity, see Barbara Fraser "A Theology Rooted in Balance," *National Catholic Reporter*, July 22, 2011.

3 www.catholicnewsagency.com/news/pope-francis-latin-america-needs-a-new-catholic-presence-in-politics-50267. The pope added that "A new

presence of Catholics in politics is necessary in Latin America."
4 www.thebubble.com/papal-politics-reading-between-the-lines-of-macris-rift-with-pope-francis/
5 https://journals.sagepub.com/doi/10.1177/0169796X04050957
6 The absurdly malign charges were made by a logger being investigated for defrauding the government https://reporterbrasil.org.br/2019/03/brazil-bolsonaro-supporter-works-to-imprison-dorothy-stangs-successor-2/ www.ncronline.org/news/world/brazilian-priest-associate-sr-dorothy-stang-arrested-brazil
7 In Columbia, Francia Marquez, a black woman, survived an attack with grenades(2019) for leading the defense of Colombian rural communities from the environmental effects caused by gold mining companies. www. telesurenglish. net/news/Colombian-Environmental-Activist-Woman-Survives-Armed-Attack-20190507-0016.html
8 Kenneth Aman, "Fighting for God: the Military and Religion in Chile," www.jstor.org/stable/24459104
9 Stephen P. Judd, "The Indigenous Theology Movement in Latin America," in *Resurgent Voices in Latin America*, edited by Edward L. Cleary and Timothy J. Steigenga (New Brunswick: Rutgers Univ. Press, 2004) 210-30.
10 Judd, ibid, 217. The splendid Baroque-style Jesuit church in Cusco (the ancient capital of the Inca Empire), was reconstructed in 1668 after being badly damaged in an earthquake in 1650. Next to the church, stands the Jesuit Univ. of San Ignacio de Loyola. Paradoxically, the two institutions were major rivals at the end of the 17th century. It was a sign of the Jesuit attempt to integrate the Incan culture. Cusco, known as the cultural capital of Peru is the oldest living city in the Americas, having been inhabited for over 3,000 years,
11 On the roles Bergoglio played as Jesuit provincial and as Archbishop and his stress on economic justice as well as his decision to hold his membership in the conservative Communion and Liberation group and on his allegedly having abandoned two left-wing Jesuit priests, who were threatened by Argentina's dictator Gen. Jorge Videla—and his being vindicated of that charge: https://aryanskynet. wordpress.com/ 2015/ 09/26/neoliberalization-theology/, and www.clarin.com/pope-francis/bergoglio-witness-the-esma-supertrial_0_H1Prwg9swQe.html
12 Judd, "The U.S. Catholic Missionary Movement on the eve of the 1997 Synod." Pope John Paul II's call for the Synod had provoked much soul-

searching and many discussions. In preparation for it, Judd had written that a consensus had been reached that it was an "opportune occasion to reflect on a shared history of solidarity and collaboration as well as an often stormy relationship marked by conflict and suspicion. No sector within the North American church should welcome this development more than the U.S. missionary movement - past, present and future. From the perspective of this movement." https://sedosmission.org/old/eng/stephen.htm

13 Gustavo Guttierez, *Revised introduction to A Theology of Liberation*, 1988, xxix. A central thesis of Marxism is that religion, Christianity included, contributes to social injustice. Liberation theology says the opposite. It says that faith and God's love oppose injustice. Gutierrez insists that human beings and ending poverty are his chief concern.

14 Gustavo Gutierrez, *A Theology of Liberation: History, Politics and Salvation*. 15th Anniversary Edition, with a new introduction by the author. Orbis Books, 1988.

15 Gutierrez, ibid, 223. Here Gutierrez is analyzing the possible shortcomings of political theology in Europe.

16 Lonergan, "The Role of a Catholic University in the Modern World," *Collection*, 109.

17 Dennis Gunn, *Religious Education*, 113, 2018, 26-37, www.tandfonline.com/doi/abs/10.1080/00344087.2017.1393179?scroll=top&needAccess=true&journalCode=urea20 Pope Francis has appointed Brazilian Cardinal Claudio Hummes as General Rapporteur for the Synod of Bishops' assembly on the Amazon. The meeting is to take place in Rome from Oct. 6 to 27, 2019, on the theme "Amazonia, new paths for the Church and for an integral ecology.

18 Lonergan, *Method in Theology*, 264. For Lonergan, being liberated from our biases depends on God's grace and on cosmopolis which refers to the links between *cosmos*, the order of nature or the universe, and *polis*, the order of human society. See John Raymaker and Godefroid Mombula, *Bringing Bernard Lonergan Down to Earth and into Our Hearts and Communities* (Wipf and Stock, 2018), 7, 12, 23, 87.

19 Raymaker, Mombula, *Bringing Bernard Lonergan Down to Earth* discusses these issues from interfaith, intercultural viewpoints. Too often, political officials are in league with the wealthy—resulting in governments of, by and for the rich run by narcissistic sociopaths who manipulate by feigning interest in people while faking both sympathy and conscience without being able to closely identify with the emotional

experience of others. See www.psychologytoday.com/us/blog/beastly-behavior/201812/the-evolutionary-role-narcissistic-sociopaths

20 Lonergan's writings can help one relate one's "inner self" with other persons within communities. See Raymaker, Mombula, *Bringing Bernard Lonergan Down to Earth*, 25-30.

21 Gustavo Gutierrez, *We Drink from our Own Wells*, (Orbis, 1984), develops a spirituality which grows out of the lived experience of the Latin American people.

CHAPTER 7

Compassionate Ways to Heal and Create in Asia

After an account of Christian healing in South Korea, we touch on the Church's delicate status in China. We then explore Bede Griffiths and Thomas Merton's creative ways of addressing interfaith issues.

Asian Liberation (*Minjung*) Theology as Pioneered in South Korea

South Korea's *Minjung* theology stresses the healing-creative aspects of encountering God and dealing with *han*. Han refers to the suffering people and communities have undergone due to unjust systems such as racism, patriarchy, and colonialism. *Minjung* theology seeks to free people from the wounds *han* has caused—wounds so deep that only the creative Spirit could bring healing.[1] In an article entitled "They'll Know We Are Christians by Our *Jeong*," Grace Ji-Sun Kim describes ways to experience the Holy Spirit with the cultural sensitivities of South Korean Christians. She speaks of her experience as a child when she first saw her mother and other people lying "on the floor weeping and shaking uncontrollably. I saw my mother, illuminated in the yellow sanctuary light—she stood upright with her hands high above her head, closed and tears rolling down her face as she spoke in tongues."[2] During the early stages of her career, Ms Kim began to reflect on how one's cultural heritage is essential if one is to understand the religious landscape "in a globalizing world where cultures clash, immigrants come together, and refugees seek new homes away from home." Ibid. The vital force of *chi* and *jeong* can help us do so. They have connoted a sense of spirituality in East Asia long before it had sustained contact with Europeans. *Chi* is close in meaning to *ruah*, the term used in both testaments of the Bible for life-giving Spirit. *Jeong* permeates the lives of Koreans; it is part of what gives joy and meaning to people's lives. It captures the essence of affection between people. It is sticky and inseparable, like honey . . .. This sticky kind of love is difficult to untangle or separate from oneself; it thus makes us stay connected to one another. Even though you may argue or fight with your friend, spouse, or family member, *jeong* will bring you back together. This is because *jeong* can be tied in to the realities of spiritual life that reminds us of our connectedness to one another, to the Spirit, and to God. We cannot live alone; we live in community and "require *jeong* to help us form bonds. . . and feelings of love and being loved." (Ibid).

Korea's *jeong* culture is communal. The personal is de-emphasized so as to build on the connectedness of people. It is akin to African tribal feeling—one that the West would do well to learn anew. Such a sense of community can help us recognize that the Holy Spirit is in relation to the other two Persons in the Trinity. Western individualism obfuscates the meaning of community in the Trinity, but the East reminds us of its importance. The Asian communal culture can enrich the West's concept of community and togetherness exemplified in the Trinity. Asian liberation theology tries to address suffering so as to free us from oppressive systems. To the extent it succeeds, one can create a more just society. *Han* (a dull ache of the soul) can open us up to a deeper understanding of the Holy Spirit—it is really the Spirit who seeks to liberate us from suffering. The Spirit is the Comforter, Counselor, and Sustainer who helps relieve us of pain and work when building a more equitable and just society. The Spirit is the Liberator who can heal our deepest wounds and bring wholeness to our broken lives. From this brief account, we can readily deduce that *Minjung* theology is just as focused on conscientization as has been Pope Francis.

The Historically Fragile Situation of the Church[3] in China

The Church of the East or Nestorian Church was present and active in China from the 7th through the 10th century, and later during the Mongol Yuan Dynasty in the 13th and 14th centuries. Locally, the religion was known as *Jingjiao/Ching-chiao* (景教), that is, the "Luminous Religion." In 1549, St. Francis Xavier, after breaking new ground for the Church Malacca in India (1545-58), visited Japan. Due to the difficulties with the Japanese reluctance to accept Christianity, he decided to travel to China for he thought that the Japanese would be more open to Christian doctrine if the Chinese had already accepted it. Unfortunately, he died one day after reaching China (near present-day Hong Kong). The Italian Matteo Ricci (1558-1610) is one of the founding figures of the Jesuit China missions. By adopting the language and culture of the country, he gained entrance to the interior of China, which was normally closed to foreigners. In 1601, Ricci was finally allowed to live in Beijing. His work there with Chinese scholars has been well publicized both in China and in the West. In recent years, the number of Chinese Christians has grown to 67 million. Christianity has grown considerably in China at an average annual rate of 7% , but the divisions between the government-approved Catholic Patriotic Church and the Church led by Vatican-appointed bishops have led to problems. In a deal with the Chinese government in September, 2018, Pope Francis recognized the legitimacy of seven bishops appointed by the Chinese government. He lifted an order that had excommunicated them. Previously, the fate of those bishops and the question of who gets to appoint new bishops in the country had been impassable barriers. The Chinese Cardinal Zen criticized the deal for it "sends the flock into the mouths of the wolves. It is a 'betrayal.'"[4] Needless to say, the role of the Church in China has been very fragile. Many cultural and political bridges must still be crossed. That will not be easy, and for that reason others have joined Cardinal Zen in their criticism.

What the Bridge-Builder Bede Griffiths Learned from Hinduism

We have noted that some reproach Christians for their roles in Europeans' empire-building. But, let us not forget that some missionaries did condemn colonialist excesses.[5] Further, as with Ricci, missionaries took initiatives in India, Tibet, and Japan to promote East-West dialogue. Bede Griffiths (1906-1993), a Benedictine monk, wrote extensively on Hinduism. Living in ashrams[6] in South India, he became a noted yogi. His writings include theological evaluations of several Hindu traditions—some of which changed over the years. He was most fascinated by *Advaita Vedanta* which differs in many ways from conventional Christian theology.[7] Griffiths was an early pioneer of interfaith dialogue, but his work was more of an encounter with Hindu beliefs than with Hindu believers. "His theology is based on the understanding of a common mystery referred to by all the world religions, a notion which may be at odds with the very premises of *Vedanta*." (Ibid, 3). Griffiths did have his limitations. In his writings, *Vedanta* refers to a variety of distinct traditions based on ideas found in the *Upanishads* and the *Bhagavad Gita*. However, he mostly depends on interpreters who base themselves "on the very ancient *Vedas, Upanishads*, and *Gita* (all translated), or the very modern and westernized Hindu sources such as Ramakrishna, and Vivekananda, who usually wrote in English. He shows little familiarity with the vast majority of Hindu theologians of the intervening two millennia."[8] Nevertheless, he remains a pioneer bridge-builder, a glocal mystic, who has enlarged, deepened the vision of many seekers for the truth.

Mystic-Glocal Bridge-Building with Thomas Merton and Pope Francis—Enlightening Westerners[9]

Robert Ellsberg argues that Thomas Merton is a modern prodigal son. Having learned his Father's lesson, he began to spiritually enlighten others. Ellsberg quotes an 18th century Jesuit on Providence: "The Holy Spirit writes no more Gospels except in our hearts. All we do from moment to moment is live this new gospel of the Holy Spirit. We, if we are holy, are the paper; our sufferings and our actions are the ink. The workings of the Holy Spirit are his pen, and with it he writes a living Gospel."[10] This is an appropriate way to describe our own project of trying to build heartfelt bridges in the manner of Pope Francis. Merton had recognized the importance of Asian-Buddhist spirituality long before the Second Vatican Council did. He realized that words cannot define the infinite-yet-unified complexity of the divine. One best avoids this dilemma by stressing the spiritual[11] and integrating it with the communal dimensions of life. Both Merton and Pope Francis have let the Holy Spirit write in their hearts with a view to help others. Ellsberg stresses Merton's encounter with Gandhi as a turning point in his life.[12] It is not enough to recount the long list of Merton's publications. One must read Merton in the light of the gospel—endeavoring to discern how his story relates to the story that God tells us through Jesus. The story of Jesus "is not just a list of his teachings or glorious mysteries—whether walking on water or raising Lazarus. It is also a story of brokenness, abandonment, and sorrow." (Ellsberg, 341). When he later began to explore Zen Buddhism, Merton found a resonance between Zen and the Desert Fathers. Like Zen *roshi's*,[13] the Desert Fathers practiced "losing self" so as to merge it into a larger reality that transcends self and object. They even used an equivalent of Zen *koans* (challenging, puzzling riddles) to teach young monks how to meditate on the emptying of Christ (*kenosis*). Seeking to empty self and to accept suffering struck Merton as akin to Buddhist "Emptiness."[14] He refers to the Thomistic doctrine of analogy by which it is just as legitimate to say that God is non-being as to affirm He is being—inasmuch as God so transcends our notions of being that any attribution of being to God is misleading. This corresponds with the mystical tradition of "un-knowing." Speaking as a monk and not as a writer, Merton said, I am happier with 'Emptiness' when I do not have to talk about it." (Coleman, ibid).

For both Buddhism and Christianity, suffering is not a "problem that one should stand outside of so as to control it;"[15] it is part of our very ego-identity and empirical existence. "The only thing to do about it is to plunge right into the middle of contradiction and confusion in order to be transformed by what Zen calls 'the great death' and Christianity calls 'dying and rising with Christ.'" (Ibid). Merton epitomizes Christian "ventures" into a glocal spirituality. He died in Bangkok after having visited India and Sri Lanka. He had spent three successive days conversing with the Dalai Lama who observed that "he had met for the first time a Christian spiritual man who opened his own eyes to what could be learned also by Buddhism from the west." For the two men, Buddhist-Christian dialogue, far from being a facile syncretism, *demands that one honestly respects* the important differences. It is during this final trip to Asia that Merton asserted that Karl Marx's main principle of "From each according to his ability, to each according to his need" forms the very basis of monastic living. Almost 20 years after Merton's death, a group of fifty Buddhist and Catholic monks met at Merton's monastery—under the Dalai Lama's direction—to discuss prayer and communal life, the stages in the process of spiritual development, and the spiritual goals of personal and social transformation.[16] Pope Francis' insistence on mercy parallels the calls of Buddhists and Merton for a world peace that deemphasizes predatory egos.[17]

Let us put this in context. During the Renaissance, Europe sought to be born anew. This led to the Enlightenment which could have been *better enlightened* if it had had notions of Buddhist enlightenment and had not forgotten the meaning of Christ's crucifixion and of the Good News of the gospels. That forgetfulness provoked the excesses of the Industrial Revolution to which Marx reacted. Merton and Pope Francis, two thoughtful glocal mystics, have stressed spiritual insights into the meaning of the Cross and of the Good News as a starting point for leading realistic lives in a confused, materialist age.[18] Jesus taught us to *pray* lest we fall into temptation. Predators *prey* on others. Jesus' kenosis on the Cross should remind us that an ethical spirituality is needed lest humans become predators. Pope Francis has realized the implications. We turn to examine how some dedicated Christians—young[19] and not so young—have been trying to be realistic-idealist apostles in our age. To be realistic-idealist Christian apostles in our age, one must be helped by supportive glocal communities in a conflicted world.

Notes

1 Ahn Byung Mu (1922-1996) pioneered *Minjung* theology. As South Korea has grown to be more economically stable since the '70s, recent theologians have re-evaluated the question of who are the poor and oppressed. Although *Minjung* theology means "people theology,"

referring to people who are poor, it does not have recourse to Marxian dogma. See also Peter Phan, *Asian Christianities: History, Theology, Practice*, (Orbis, 2018).

2 Grace Ji-Sun Kim, on *Jeong*, in "Five Asian concepts that can deepen our understanding of the Holy Spirit." https://sojo.net/biography/grace-ji-sun-kim 12-28-2018. *Jeong* is feeling, love, sentiment, passion, human nature, sympathy, heart. The location of *jeong* is between individuals. http://www.prcp.org/publications/sig.pdf

3 China has sent hundreds of thousands of the ethnic-Muslim Uyghurs in Xinjiang to "re-education" camps. See https://international.la-croix.com/news/china-leads-the-way-in-religious-persecution/9062

4 www.theguardian.com/world/2018/sep/22/vatican-pope-francis-agreement-with-china-nominating-bishops

5 C. W. Forman, "The Growth of the study of the expansion of Christianity." *Religious Studies Review* 13 (1). Bartolomé de las Casas, a 16th-century Spanish colonist, spent 50 years of his life actively fighting slavery.

6 *Ashram* is the usually secluded abode where a guru and his disciples practice penance and the austerities of a spiritual life. It facilitates the spirit of prayer and occasional solitude Christians need. It can also refer to any of the four spiritual abodes or stages of life that the "twice born" will ideally pass. One passes through the stages of student, householder (requiring marriage and family), hermit and the homeless mendicant. Buddha underwent these stages prior being enlightened. These stages offer ideals for those in search of spiritual solutions. But Christianity today must also learn to guide its followers in the complex ways of modern society so that its properly enlightened followers may be able to uplift our alienated society and change it for the better if possible. Judith Walter was one of Dom Bede's closest companions. She has spent most of her adult life in Asia and Africa. She often went to Dom Bede's Shantivanam *ashram* for contemplative practice. In the House of Prayer in Tanzania, she now offers hospitality and provides for the spiritual needs of those seeking spiritual renewal.

7 Pål W. Thorbjørnsen, *A Christian Vedanta? Bede Griffiths and the Hindu-Christian Encounter.*

8 Robert Fastiggi and Jose Pereira, "The Swami from Oxford." *Crisis* (March 1991), 22-25.

9 On how Joseph de Maistre picked up on Rousseau's critique of the Enlightenment, see "Rousseau, Maistre and the Counter Enlightenment."

https://www.jstor.org/stable/26214387?seq=1#page_scan_tab_contents. That Pope Francis is a glocal mystic, the conscience of the world, is clear from his occasional chiding members of the Roman Curia, including its Cardinals, for certain remediable shortcomings—as in the film "A Man of his Word." Our term "glocal mystic" reinforces the faith-belief distinction; a "mystic" lives within the "*faith*-orbit" of an eye of love.

10 Jean-Pierre de Caussade, *Abandonment to Divine Providence*. For Ellsberg, Merton is a modern prophet. See Ellsberg, http://merton.org/ITMS/Annual/19/Ellsberg340-354.pdf.

11 Paradoxically, this dilemma helps relate the three world religions in that all of their mystics acknowledge the limitation of words as to the Ultimate. But since humans need words to communicate, the experience of God is paraphrased in "*beliefs*" which help unite the believers of a given religion but separate them from other religions.

12 Gandhi found "a congenial 'second home in Jesus' Sermon on the Mount." John A. Coleman, "Thomas Merton," America, *The Jesuit Review* 98. July 13, 2012, 5. Catholicism and Buddhism both have a middle way to enlighten a person so that "the incredible becomes credible." For Gandhi and Pope Francis similarities: www.peterlang.com/view/9783653975147/part2.html. On Merton's limitations, see https://catholicherald.co.uk dailyherald/2019/04/10/thomas-mertons-illicit-affair-and-the-weakness-of-sixties-zen-catholicism/ One psychiatrist told Merton, "You want a hermitage in Times Square with a large sign over it saying 'hermit,'"; we stress that Merton was a prophet.

13 *Roshi* is the Japanese honorific title used for highly venerated senior teachers in Zen Buddhism.

14 Buddhist Emptiness refers to the vast, interconnected webs of internally related networks—a teaching that we approach from a faith-mystic perspective making the needed distinctions.

15 In *Zen Masters*, ix, Merton writes that Zen is "a lived ontology which explains itself not" theoretically, but "in acts emerging out of a certain quality of consciousness and awareness. Only by these acts and by this quality of consciousness can Zen be judged." For him, Zen and Christianity are compatible. In its essence, Buddhism is about suffering, its causes and the paths to live with yet beyond it. It is about emptiness (the delusion of a subject-object distinction and the non-substantiality and transient nature of all existence). It is also about universal compassion." Both Merton and D. T. Suzuki, https://terebess.hu/zen/mesterek/d-t-suzuki-mysticism-christian-and-buddhist.pdf,

wrote on approaching God apophatically (without words) as the void, as emptiness transcending subject and object, in "pure darkness" (the dark night of the soul and of the senses of St. John of the Cross). The pure void and pure light come together. Merton cites some enigmatic remarks by 1) John of the Cross on *todo y nada* (everything and nothing at once!); 2) the mystic Jacob Boehme: "God is called the seeing and finding of the Nothing and, therefore, is called a nothing (though it is God himself) because it is inconceivable and inexpressible;" 3) Meister Eckhart in which Merton found affinities to Zen: "To be a proper abode for God and fit for God to act in, a man should also be free from all things and actions, both inwardly and outwardly." See Coleman, 5.

16 Donald Mitchell and James Wiseman, eds. *Gethsemani Encounter New York, Continuum*, vii. A Buddhist monk endorsed Merton's remark: "At the center of our being is a point of nothingness which is untouched by sin and by illusion, a point of pure truth, a point or spark which belongs entirely to God, . . . from which God disposes of our lives." Coleman, 2012, 5. That spark is inaccessible to the fantasies of our minds or to the brutalities of the world.

17 Buddhists speak of mindfulness—being awake to the present moment and in touch with those around you. It complements Christian Centering Prayer which has updated early Christians' contemplative practices as well as the practices described in the 14th century classic *The Cloud of Unknowing*, or by Christian mystics such as John Cassian, Francis de Sales, Teresa of Avila, John of the Cross. Recall Jesus' words: "When you pray, go to your inner room, close the door and pray to your Father in secret. Your Father, who sees in secret, will repay you." (Matt 6:6).

18 Merton, *No Man is an Island* (New York, Harcourt, 1955), 92: "To know the Cross is not merely to know our own sufferings. For the Cross is the sign of salvation, and no man is saved by his own sufferings. To know the Cross is . . . to know the love of Christ." For the pope, Jesus' death is immersed in an atmosphere of prayer. Jesus consoles the women, prays for His crucifiers, promises Paradise to the good thief, expires saying: "Father, into thy hands I commit my spirit!" (Luke 23:46). Jesus' prayer would deaden the most violent emotions and desires of revenge. It would have us reconcile ourselves with enemies. https://zenit.org/articles/pope-proposes-persistence-in-prayer/

19 See https://www.taize.fr/en on the many young people who trek every year to Taize for spiritual renewal.

Part THREE
Pioneering Effective Christian Ministries in a Divided, Conflicted World

CHAPTER 8

New Forms of Community and Ministries in the Age of Pope Francis

Some Remarkable Bridging-Conscientization Processes Occurring in the Church

Pope Francis is not naïve as he builds bridges. He "endorses" glocal-relational[1] theologies that unite rather than divide the world. Growing depersonalization in urban areas and the rise of authoritarian regimes have provoked political, cultural and religious strife across the globe. Francis has staked his papacy and the future of the Catholic Church on attempts to mediate such multifaceted strife. He *is* the conscience of the world—deliberately reaching out to all. He encourages Latin America's *conscientization* process urged by liberation theology,[2] in which Small Christian Communities (SCC's) play a role. He promotes the joy of the Gospel despite the resistance[3] he meets along the way. It is no small feat! In 2013, the pope met with Gustavo Gutierrez, the founder of liberation theology and Cardinal Gerhard Müller,[4] then Prefect of the Church's doctrinal congregation. He said that critics of liberation theology overreact when they condemn all Central American Jesuits without distinction.[5] Upon asking a Central American bishop about the pending sainthood cause of Archbishop Romero, the bishop replied: "Do not even speak of it! It would be like canonizing Marxism!"[6] The reality is that the yeast of the Gospel has been at work within the Latin American Church over the past 50 years, largely due to the 1968 Medellin Bishops' Conference. Until then, the Latin America Church had operated in neo-colonialist ways which had dominated the continent until Vatican II set in. Inspired by Gutierrez, the Latin American Church began a process of decolonization by reforming its structures. A key element in this reformation was the development of Basic Christian Communities (BBC's) also known as *Communidades de Base*. This reflects the compelling need today for loving communities that can re-awaken Christians. Don Quixote lamented the loss of Christian ideals; Joseph Conrad pointed to the dark colonialist excesses. Like Cervantes and Conrad, Pope Francis knows what ails Western Christianity. He is aware of possible BBC-SSC solutions.[7]

Relating the Thought and Foundations of BBC's and SSC's to Actual Societal Needs

Political problems today are no longer addressed from faith perspectives. Theologians and sociologists have been re-examining the original structures of the Church. They have come to realize that SSC's played vital roles in the early Church.[8] These could again play crucially vital roles in modern societies to the extent they could enable the faithful to live the faith more intimately within church structures. Recent popes have encouraged the growth of BCC's and SCC'S. They realize, in principle, that BBC's and SSC's embody viable ways to live the Good News in age of unprecedented changes. In the secularized West, few attend Sunday Mass. Among those who do, the Eucharist does not affect Catholics' basic convictions. Too often, that experience only reinforces already held views of what life is all about. Only those who do not rush home after attending Mass so as to reflect and share in deeper ways such as in SCC's are able to truly live Christian lives. Are local bishops willing to effect glocal parish renewals today?

The renewal of the Liturgy effected at Vatican II has energized some, but alienated others. Vatican II reforms have also opened new perspectives for Christian participation in the world. But if the Vatican and traditionalist bishops seek to micro-manage the laity, they risk snuffing out the spirit of renewal. Vatican II recognized people's basic needs for intimacy, for reading Scripture in ways that can help transform communities. Clericlay cooperation could open up new forms of ministries able to reach out to a secularized culture and to believers in various religions as well. Establishing God's Kingdom on earth includes subordinating Church structures to Kingdom imperatives. For over 200 years, Western society has been conscious of alienated people living on the margins of a faceless, industrialized society. BBC's and SCC's provide ways to fulfill people's need for intimacy. The one, holy, catholic, apostolic Church can flourish anew in BBC-SCC's. This could help unify the Church—not divide it—since BBC-SSC's can open new ways of interacting in apostolic ways in keeping with the Church's traditional ways of bridge-building. In principle, both the BBC's of Latin America and the SSC's active in other parts of the world follow the example of the apostolic Church: "They devoted themselves to the apostles' instruction… and prayer." (Acts 2:42). BBC-SSC's appeal to those who love the Church and want to evangelize. Their origins and aims do differ in some respects, but they all provide ways for Christians[9] today to live their calling authentically. We shall first examine Latin American BBC's, and then SSC's in Africa and in the USA.

The Roles of BBC's in Latin America

The influx of immigrants has affected the ministries of Latin America's BBC's. This influx has led to the need of specialized BBC formation. BBC's are small, homogeneous groups whose members gather to read and reflect on Scripture. Three core elements define BBC's: a striving for small community; a stress on ecclesial linkage; ongoing links to societal structures. Yet, BBC's are seen as "suspect" by some clerics and the dominant class. BCCs are not anti-parish, being indirectly linked to a parish. Tension arises when a pastor wants to intrude. BBC's believe that it is better to decide in ways that involve the laity.[10] The development of BBC's in Latin America has largely focused on those lacking a voice, those at the bottom of the socioeconomic structure. Gustavo Gutierrez's writings on liberation theology and Paulo Freire's *Pedagogy of the Oppressed* have both played key roles in liberating people from oppression and in the formation of BBC's. Some BBC's help train leaders who then see to it that the voices of the poor and oppressed are heard. Freire helped train thousands of BBC leaders to implement his method in Brazil. "Education either functions as an instrument to integrate the younger generation into the logic of the present system and bring about conformity or it becomes the practice of freedom, the means by which men and women deal critically with reality" so as to "transform the world."[11] Freire helped actualize the option for the poor embraced by Latin American bishops at Medellin in 1968. The ensuing increase of BBC's in Brazil and Central America, gave Church conservatives pretexts to claim that liberation theology and BBC's lean toward Marxism. Given the fear of communism, many missionaries in Latin America[12] were caught up in such conflicts for several decades. The canonization of St. Oscar Romero highlighted the Church's embracing the cause of the poor and the need to confront social injustice. In his 2013 message to Brazil, Pope Francis endorsed BBC's, linking their roles in evangelization to what he had written in *Joy of the Gospel*. BBC's are Pilgrims of the Kingdom calling members to fulfill the Church's mission. They are an instrument for helping people learn God's Word so as to commit themselves to Gospel values in new forms of lay service and adult education in the faith" (178). For the pope, BBC's "bring a new evangelizing fervor and a new capacity for dialogue with the world whereby the Church is renewed." They must "not lose contact with the rich reality of the local parish." (29). Evangelization is a duty of the whole Church: we are all pilgrims, in the countryside and in the city, bringing the joy of the Gospel to every man and woman. The pope recalled the words of St. Paul, "Woe to me if I do not preach the Gospel!" (1 Cor 9:16). This should resound in the hearts of all. He invited BBC's to walk with Jesus, proclaiming and witnessing to the poor the prophecy of a "new heaven and a new earth."[13]

The Development and Roles of SSC's in Africa and in the USA

Joseph Healey has highlighted the role of Small Christian Communities (SCC's).[14] He has helped establish a clearinghouse on SCC activities throughout the world. Relying on the theologian Brian Hearne, he encourages the formation of SCC's because they offer a form of spirituality that is in touch with the African temperament—a theme that has been developed, for instance, by George Gichuhi.[15] For Gichuhi, the African value of community is expressed in the conviction of the fundamental African proverb "I am because we are; we are because I am." SCCs can be described as "truly African, truly Christian." The spirituality of SCCs is rooted in Jesus's commandment of love and service. SCC members in Africa live out their African Christian spirituality by reaching out to others, especially the poor and needy. In their service to the community, African SCCs strive to integrate African values with gospel values.

In the USA, SCC's seek to respond to the changing nature of our glocal civilization. They largely function within existing Church structures. Generally speaking, fostering communal living has both sociological and spiritual implications. Many Christians today take part in diverse communities at their workplace, school, or in their neighborhood. In many Western urban centers, the local parish is no longer the primary community of devoted Christians. This is due to the use of technology and social media which facilitates the growth of virtual communities. For instance, a SCC in Northern California, *La Communidad de Ministerios Christianos* (the Community of Christian Ministries) has been active for forty years. Like other SCC's, it facilitates biblical reflection. From its inception in 1978, it has met twice each month in member's homes—in accord with St. Paul's words (I Tim: 3:15): "The Church is called God's family." Members support the homeless, help addicts,[16] and immigrants. Some members work with Maryknoll Affiliates;[17] others participate in the social justice ministries of the San Jose Diocese. *La Communidad*, now part of a network of over 20 SSC's in California, combines a biblical spirituality with social justice outreach. These SCC's interact with one another through the Zoom network to discuss issues of mutual concern such as spirituality and justice. SCCs can be an effective vehicle for reaching out to men and women without access to traditional parish structures. Lay ministries need to be created which can bring the Gospel to homeless encampments that now exist within most urban areas of the world.

Some Possible Roles for SCC's in the USA Including Adequate Responses to Marginalization

Most people see parishes as the smallest unit of Church organization, but the lack of priests and other realities call for renewed Church structures that can foster genuine SCC's. In large parishes in which only the voices of the pope, the bishop and parish priest count, the real aim of assembling Christians to pray and build community is defeated. Westerners tend to think in terms of organization and task-oriented groups, rather than in environmental/communal terms. Many well-known SSC advocates argue that parishes should subordinate structure to community. The Church's hierarchic structure has been one of its strengths, yes, for no organization, however small, can survive if no one is in charge. But there are formal and informal ways of being organized. Parishes thrive by being formally organized. SCC's flourish through their informal approach to ministry. SCC advocates speak of "restructuring" the Church. We argue that incarnational-relational[18] theologies and spiritualities can help restructure the Church.

"Whoever pursues righteousness and love finds life, prosperity and honor." (*Proverbs*, 21, 21). This ideal does not always obtain in reality, but it is pursued by many SCC's. In the face of rugged individualism, SSC's foster living in communities such as in intentional communities, eco-village and housing co-operatives. Such communities restore forms of intimacy, enabling members to share in the midst of a secularized, depersonalized world. The Church has a rich tradition of community life embodied in its religious orders of men and women such as the Benedictines, Dominicans and Franciscans. While there is now a diminished commitment to religious life on the part of youth, there is also an ever-increasing need for viable forms of community life in secular societies. Many of the world's problems will remain intractable without effective means to work out solutions. Too often, government programs fail due to mismanagement, greed or graft. Volunteers are often not adequately supported. NGO's partly fill the vacuum between government inefficiency and personal limitations. The prejudices within one's heart due to consumerist addictions may blind one to the needs of others. SCC's help individual Christians and the glocal Church engage in "intimate" forms of joint apostolates to counter both depersonalized and individualistic societal attitudes.[19] SCC members share and reflect on personal experiences. Some focus on the social justice mission of the Church and its prophetic role in society. Conscientization of the oppressed is now part of the Church's mission. SCC's as part of the glocal Church can help catalyze social transformations. Just as religious orders have traditionally played a role auxiliary to the Church's hierarchy, so we envision SCC's as also playing such an auxiliary role with an appropriate canonical basis. John Paul II made Opus Dei a "praelatio nullius" so that it is directly subject to the pope. SCC's can be auxiliaries with various modes of "flexible" types of accountability to the Church hierarchy. Pope Francis' support of SSC's is a step in the right direction to get people involved in them to meet various needs.

Marginalization in society—even in the Church—are indirectly addressed in Jesus' parables. The parable of the Good Samaritan concludes that everyone is my neighbor (Lk 10, 25-37). Other parables in Luke stress that Jesus came to save the "lost." "Getting lost" in today's global society touches on the reality that migrants must either learn a new language— or create new "ghettos." When it comes to renewing the Church, only the language of love will do. The shortage of priests and religious makes SCC's almost indispensable means for compensating for that fact. SCC's could help more in educating the young or foster spirituality. Although SSCs in the USA have been spared the confrontations that greeted Latin America's BBC's, they still await official Church recognition. It is clear that the Church is often out of date in that it has not fully responded to pressing issues and problems nor enlisted the help of SCC'S. Vatican II's "Decree on the Bishops' Pastoral Office in the Church," repeats over and over again that the welfare of the "flock" must be the first priority in governing a diocese. SCCs within parish and diocesan structures have been "successful" but neither the laity nor priests will feel empowered if they can be all too arbitrarily silenced when venturing into new territory such as engaging in social justice ministries. "Since the role of the priest is primarily that of a credible witness, it is of the utmost importance that all Church structures, all basic relationships within the Church, and the whole of moral formation promote and encourage absolute sincerity and transparency."[20] Glocal cooperation is needed to do this.

Clericalism is now a problem in Catholicism. The naming and firing of bishops rests with the Pope. Many recent Church scandals and their coverup, Pope Francis has had to revise norms of conduct meant to prevent practices that led to the abuse[21] of power by clerics. The Western churches should learn from the insights of Africans and Asians into the spiritual life. One should do more than just attend Sunday Mass if one is to live a more authentic Christian life. Outlines for new types of Christian mission—living holy, (holistic) lives in our secular world—do exist in Church teachings. But due to the dysfunctions affecting both the world and the Church, an effective coordination for living holy lives has tended to be put on a back burner. Many tragic events such as the wars going on many parts of the world, the proliferation of new technologies, and the clergy sexual abuse scandals have had telling consequences for the Church. Many Catholic religious orders are now facing financial crises, being unable to attract new members even though they have increasing numbers of aged and infirm retirees to support. The future of Catholicism may partly rest with new forms of BBC-SCC's now growing on the Church's periphery. Pope Francis. realizing the need for a spiritual renewal of the Church, has linked that need with a structural renewal of the Church. We shall briefly address this twofold need by considering the plight of young Christians who feel alienated in the Church. Can their plight be alleviated, for instance, through emergent forms of dual-belonging—to the Church and to a Buddhist spirituality, for instance?

The Plight of Many Young Christians Feeling Alienated in the Church

Many young people feel alienated from traditional church structures. They no longer identify with a particular faith tradition but view themselves as seekers after spiritual experiences not restricted to a particular belief. They want to share in authentic, spiritual experiences that can help them encounter the divine and avoid being isolated using hi-tech gadgets. Humans were never meant to be solitary so many young people seek new ways to serve humanity. Since new wine must not be poured into old wine skins, some SCC's have reached out to the youth, helping them participate in the phenomenon of "dual religious belonging."[22] A further recent development is the changing roles of women's religious communities which has seen some of them abandon their traditional roles in Catholic hospitals and schools in favor of more outreach into the communities where they live. They serve the needs of the homeless, immigrants, and those living on the margins of society. One such new role is espoused by "Nuns and Nones Unite." What began as a series of conversations between Catholic nuns and non-affiliated millennials ("Nones"), evolved into a communal experiment in Burlingame, CA.[23] Dominican Sister Gloria Jones summarizes the "changing mission of her community. Today the critical human need is related to community, to a spiritual quest, to finding meaning." (Ibid). This trend is part of a wider effort of women religious to find new ways[24] to reach the younger generation and form new bonds with them. Approximately one-third of the millennial generation now considers itself to be Nones—lacking any connection to a religious traditions. The decline and devolution of the Catholicism in Europe is now beginning to occur in the United States. Sharing new forms of community life with the "Nones" may be one way of renewing their interest in spirituality through dedicated SCC's.

Summarizing Thoughts on the Need for New Christian Communities such as BBC's and SSC's

How best relate existing Church structures with the wish of many Catholics to participate in community? It is a matter of priorities. Only if Christians have meaningful communities where they can discuss issues in depth with a hope of being heard can their faith flourish. Constrictive structures can snuff out faith initiatives. Being more in touch with people's needs, Church leaders can better help the faith flourish. Church structures should support small communities so that they could help charity thrive. This is possible because people who have truly experienced the grace of God gladly share that grace with others. BBC-SSC's can be a Gospel leaven, enlightening the clueless, the alienated. By listening, bishops can better guide the faithful in the Church's mission. The goal of the Church is not to have structures, but to help establish God's Kingdom on earth by living the Christian life—a point made by many who have written on BBC's and SCC's. BBC's and SCC's mostly seek to work within, not against Church structures.

Our review of SCC-BBC's has noted how they help conscientize and empower people—strengthening them in their struggle against the various forms of marginalization plaguing them. People are empowered by the dynamics of community acceptance. SCC's help Christians improve their position on the margins; they empower them by responding to their need for intimacy with new forms of ministry. Both faith and our work life are to be rooted in a sound spirituality and a sound glocal ethics. Many persons throughout the world now seek to incorporate both a spiritual foundation and an ethical vision.

Joseph Healey has outlined[25] some key biblical passages that provide a Christian spirituality for the development of many SCC's that share a common biblical source and emphasize the roles of community: *Ecclesiastes 4:9-12*: "Two are better than one, because they have a good reward for their toil. For if they fall, one will lift up the other; but woe to one who is alone and falls and does not have another to help."

Matthew 18:20: "For where two or three are gathered in my name, there I am among them."

Acts 2:42-47 depicts a model of community life: Importance of the witness of life, praying together, breaking of the bread (sharing what we have). BBC's and SCC's hold up this model as their ideal.

Acts 4:32: "the community of believers was of one mind and heart."

These passages reveal SCC's true foundation—a call to live as much as is possible as did the SSC's in *The Acts of the Apostles*. Today's SSC's are reviving a way of being church that is 2,000 years old!

The future of Christian life may rest with the formation of new types of communities that involve lay people rekindled by the Holy Spirit. It is in SCCs that Christians first experienced what the Church is in its very core; they may be the most effective way for the Church to renew itself today. SCC's can work in coordination with the Church's official structures and provide inspiration for effective renewal. In them, we find a keen appreciation of life's deeper meanings. They help its members find new forms of self-transcending intimacy in an age of hype and profit-maximization. Vatican II initiated this process. It also provided the Church with new methods for ecumenism and interfaith dialogue. Pope Francis' call for a renewal of Gospel values is taken seriously by most SSC-BBC's within the Church. Evangelization must occur at every social level to meet the needs of our contemporary, pluralistic societies. Dialogue with all is a must today for it can aid renew the Church itself. In Pope Francis' words: "Other Church institutions, basic communities and small communities . . . and forms of association enrich the Church raised up by the Spirit for evangelizing different areas and sectors. Frequently, they bring a new evangelizing fervor and a new capacity for dialogue with the world whereby the Church is renewed." (*Joy of the Gospel*, 29).

Notes

1. God, in the Bible, is thoroughly relational; many are increasingly aware of our own interrelatedness with others.
2. Recall Pope John Paul II's waving of his finger at the priest-poet Ernesto Cardenal in 1983 upon his visit to Nicaragua. A year later, the pope removed Cardenal's faculties to celebrate the sacraments publicly. In 2019, Pope Francis rehabilitated Cardenal. It is as if Pope Francis has examined the Church's conscience and the strings that tie us to the world. What makes this possible is his deep spirituality, his ability to balance secular and spiritual needs.
3. For the pope's answer to conservative Catholics who call him a heretic: www.politico.eu/article/pope-francis-heretic-vatican-liberal-conservative-war/ John Paul II, Benedict XVI and Francis were all affected by socio-political happenings. Gerald Whalen, https://jesuits.eu/news/453-understanding-pope-francis-approach, argues that a major challenge today is negotiating the transition from classical mindedness, which depends on time and space, to historical consciousness that pays heed to the particularities of a culture changing over time. As a Jesuit in Argentina, the pope had worried about potentially harmful interpretations of the preferential option for the poor.
4. In one of his books, Müller describes liberation theology as a "significant currents of Catholic theology of the 20th century" that helped the church bridge the divides between "earthly happiness and ultra-earthly salvation."
5. www.lastampa.it/2019/02/14/vaticaninsider/francis-reveals-he-concelebrated-mass-with-cardinal-muller-and-gustavo-gutierrez-Gy3CmbckabqH7jRzCMw78O/pagina.html In a question and answer session with the Jesuits in Panama, the pope quipped that if someone from decades ago had predicted that such an event would occur "they would be taken as a drunk." In fact, in 2014, Müller published a book defending liberation theology and Gutiérrez.
6. Ibid. In his January, 2019 address to the Central America churches, the pope said that many people of diverse vocations "have devoted their lives and even shed their blood to keep the Church's prophetic voice alive in the face of injustice, the spread of poverty, and the abuse of power. . .The bishops of this region were the first in America to create a means of communion and participation that continues to bear rich fruit… (providing) a forum for sharing, discernment and agreement that nurtures, revitalizes and enriches your Churches." www.vaticannews.

va)en/pope/ news/2019-01/pope-francis-panama-wyd-2019-address-bishops-central-america.html. The Document of Aparecida of 2007, authored by the future pope, notes that BBCs allow people to commit themselves to the Gospel. (No. 178).

7   If SCC's embody concrete ways for the Church to reform itself, the pope is drawing larger implications as is clear from *Laudato Si*, from his outreach to moderate Muslims and to young Christians—all in a spirit of contagious joy.

8   The early Church depended upon informal networks such as house churches; these grew into more established structures such as monasteries, communities of widows which provided services to the wider society.

9   Rick Warren started his Saddleback Church in Lake Forest, CA in 1980 with just one family. His original SCC now has hundreds of affiliates; his *The Purpose Driven Life* is an all-time best seller. He is a fan of Pope Francis.

10 Teotonio R. de Sousa, SJ., "Basic Christian Communities," *Theology Annua*, vol. 12 1990-1991, 181-201. http://archive.hsscol.org.hk/Archive/periodical/abstract/A012l.htm

11 Paulo Freire, *Pedagogy of the Oppressed*, 34. https://www.azquotes.com/author/5153-Paulo_Freire

12 Fr. Blasé Bonpane was forced to leave Maryknoll due to his support of the poor in Guatemala. He then became until his death in 2019, a strong, respected critic of U. S. militarism which he insisted is anti-democratic.

13 https://w2.vatican.va/content/francesco/en/letters/2013/documents/papa-francesco_20131217_comunita-ecclesiali-base.html. Egoists are unconcerned with others' problems. They are concerned only about themselves.

14 Healey, *Building the Church as the Family of God: Evaluation of Small Christian Communities* in East Africa: (Orbis, 2018) stresses that the primordial spiritual consciousness in Africa is rooted in music and dance. Western thought has lost much of its rootedness in ecstatic experiences. Having forgotten human rootedness, it puts us all at risk.

15 *George N. Gichuhi. The Spirituality of Small Christian Communities in Eastern Africa.* Eldoret, Kenya: Gaba (1985). He refers to Tanzanian theologian Laurenti Magesa's "How Many Loaves Do You Have? Christian Pedagogy and the African Ethos" in *Tangaza Journal of Theology and Mission* 2014/1, 28-49 who writes: "From its inception

as a community after the outpouring of the Holy Spirit at Pentecost," the New Testament church was "of one heart and mind," (Acts 4:32), sharing everything they had. To say, then, that SCCs constitute a "new way of being church" is a serious mischaracterization. The African church is rediscovering in the SCC'S the original manner of being church. See also http://smallchristiancommunities.org/wp-content/uploads/2018/04/scc_histories_themes.pdf

16 As AA and other anonymous groups help former addicts deal with their dependencies—even with their obsessions—so the Church must help Christians and humans in general deal with their false dependencies.

17 The Maryknoll Affiliates practice glocal forms of community that combine spirituality with a strong sense of solidarity with those marginalized by society. Referring to the "death of institutions," John Sivalon, MM writes that the Affiliates depend upon members' ability to live as a fluid, open movement not restricted by rules or regulations—on not being "neurotically concerned about self-preservation." The Affiliates' openness to other faiths and to those of no faith means that the hierarchical entities of the Maryknoll family do not possess it. It would touch "the hands of the other, allowing the same water of life to run over each other's hands so as to enliven all." Living the Gospel freely and spiritually can help establish God's Kingdom due to being aware of injustices across the world. See webmaster@maryknollaffiliates.org. Our glocal, ethical approach is very much in tune with these views.

18 Elaine Pagels in *Beyond Belief: The Secret Gospel of Thomas* (Vintage, 2004) argues that Irenaeus' incarnational theology left little room for any alternative claims about the relationship of Jesus' humanity with his divinity. Most of the New Testament titles for Jesus until the end of the first century were more ambiguous about Jesus' divinity such as the title of the Son of Man. Irenaeus provided a clear presentation about how Jesus could be both God and man; his teaching about heresy left little room for any alternative theology in the Jesus movement.

19 Although problems can occur in restructuring the Church, we stress the importance of communal forms of living. Christopher Hedges, www.cbc.ca/radio/ideas/christopher-hedges-farewell-america-1.4911396 says that addiction, income disparity and hollowed-out towns and cities are increasingly becoming the norm in the USA, while the political and financial sectors tend to merge with each other to the exclusion of anyone else's needs.

20 Cited by Pope Benedict XVI, http://w2.vatican.va/content/benedict-

xvi/en/speeches/2009/february/documents/hf_ben-xvi_spe_20090226_clergy-rome.html
21 The majority of priests are dedicated servants of God. Still, Francis wants to demonstrate that due to clericalism the Church is now structurally saddled with psychological, spiritual and sexual abuse. See https://international.la-croix.com/news/combating-clericalism/9969?utm_source=Newsletter&utm_medium=e-mail&utm_content=26-04-2019&utm_campaign=newsletter_crx_lci&PMID=0964dbe689e61e205168552536593154
22 Paul Knitter, *Without Buddha I Could Not Be a Christian* (Oneworld Publications, 2013).
23 *National Catholic Reporter*, February 22- March 7, 2019, 8.
24 Many admired Linda Gregg's ability to discuss grief and longing with electrifying craftsmanship and poise. Her spiritual autobiography is a search for the Ground of Being, for a condition of wholeness within the shards of time. See www.nytimes.com/2019/03/27/obituaries/linda-gregg-dead.html. Pope Francis, too, has sought wholeness.
25 http://smallchristiancommunities.org/wp-content/uploads/2018/04/scc_histories_themes.pdf

CHAPTER 9

A Global but Divided Christianity Needs Glocal Initiatives to Cope with the Future

Pope Francis is said to be the conscience of the world. He has helped people of good will glocally link global problems with local insights so as to find viable solutions. In January 2019, the pope stressed that the Word of God[1] is not ideological. It helps us grow. He asked "What does it mean for a Christian to have a perverse heart?" Take care, brothers, that none of you have a fainthearted, evil and unfaithful heart, so as to forsake the living God." He did not mince his words as he stressed that "priests, nuns, bishops also run the danger of being perverted by hardness, obstinacy and seduction."[2]

Contextualizing the Evolving Views on Sexuality in the Catholic Church

To contextualize the sexual scandals that have rocked the Church, one must focus on the Church's long history of failing to adequately address a theology of sexuality in ways that could bridge the divides between moral relativism and moral dogmatism. That failure is rooted in the Jansenist theology taught in seminaries prior to Vatican II. The present Church discipline of mandatory celibacy for priests was first imposed by the Gregorian Reform in the 11th century. We are not able to go into all of the factors that led to the recent scandals. Pope Francis is taking measures to better train aspiring priests, including psychological counseling and testing. The pope is also exploring the restoration of women deacons. The Vatican, in conjunction with specialized institutes or training centers, will need to provide resources for a periodic evaluation of priests, religious and lay ministers. In some parts of the world, consideration is now being given to the ordination of married men. The Catholic Church already has a married clergy for it has allowed married Anglican and Episcopal priests to be part its own priesthood. To contextualize such issues, we have repeatedly urged the fostering of a glocal conscience rooted in a valid spirituality.

A Glocal Ecological Conscience Motivated by and/or Promoting a Viable Glocal Spirituality

Indeed Pope Francis has set a high standard as he calls for an ecological conversion—one that is in need of a "global spirituality" linked both to common prophetic heritage of the three religions of the Book and to the insights of Eastern religions. Such a glocal spirituality could serve as a foundation for an ethic that appeals to secularists if they truly want to help relieve the plight of people in the developing world. To the extent humans overcome their divides, they can help the world deal with critical areas of life. Many of the world's problems will remain intractable unless glocal intermediary organizations[3] are in place.

Zen master Thich Nhat Hanh explains why a spiritual revolution rather than economics is needed to protect nature and limit climate change. "We have constructed a system we can't control. It imposes itself on us, and we become its slaves and victims." We have created a society in which the rich become richer and the poor become poorer, and in which we are so caught up in our own immediate problems that we are hardly aware of "what is going on with the rest of the human family or on planet Earth."[4] Thich compares humans to a group of chickens in a cage disputing over a few seeds of grain, unaware that in a few hours they will all be killed." (Ibid). Blind prejudices and uncritical assumptions of many kinds must be taken into account. In order to develop a needed sense of intimacy in life within responsible communities we need to recognize present obstacles now facing us. Indeed, the good is intertwined with evil in so many areas of life. It will take some doing for humans to realize that they can and should be guided by a glocal conscience and a truly glocal spirituality responsive to today's needs.

Dealing with the Intertwining[5] of Good and Evil in Our Lives: The Challenges the Church Faces

Pope Francis has often looked at evil (or at least at the greedy manifestations of it) in the eye.[6] He knows that good and evil get intertwined in the lives of each person, in the organizations humans devise. But this has not stopped him from being a realistic optimist for he trusts in God. Jesus taught us to "turn the other cheek." but this has to be and has been contextualized in the teaching and practice of the Church. The gospels, the Church, as well as the world religions all teach that we have to resist evil. Let us recall that the Christian genius Blaise Pascal explored the heart and its reasons. The heart's reasons are feelings that respond to values felt by persons who truly love.[7] We use short-hand phrases such as glocal mystics and a glocal eye of love to express such loving responses. Pope Francis' *Laudato Si* and his pastoral exhortations all address the dramatic problems humanity faces; they point to needed solutions. These would include a Pascal-like *eye of love* rather than a cynical *Realpolitik* Machiavellianism a la Trump or la Bolsonaro in Brazil. Both these presidents manipulate persons—leading to human disarray and environmental degradation. Good and evil are indeed intertwined in our very being and in the fabric of nations. There is a pressing need to delve into such problems and how they affect the Church.

Pope Francis has had the courage to tackle such problems. But even a pope can only do so much. Napoleon, Bismark and Stalin all mocked a pope's lack of military might—knowing they could prevail on military and political fronts. One may ask what can the Church realistically do to improve our lot? Our glocal-prophetic dialogue is contingent with the extent to which faith, hope, and love are lived—rather than being sidetracked.[8] Pope Francis is taking the bull by the horns, as it were, as he addresses the challenges facing the Church—such as those of secularity, egoism, syncretism and migrations. Pivotal to our argument is the extent to which people truly live their lives based on solid ethical foundations.[9]

Relating Religious-Mystic Experiences to Persons' Actual Ways of Living Their Lives

Humanity must avoid relativism. Pope Francis, in his outreach to other religions and to people of good will, implicitly uses the crucial faith-belief distinction we have stressed. Teaching the tenets of religion to youngsters may pit parents and teachers against the secular mentality the young have to live with. The Church's catechism refers to St. Thomas Aquinas' teaching on the mystery of the Holy Trinity, but students may say, "If one can 'know' something, it is hardly a mystery." A person's horizon broadens as one reaches toward the unknown.[10] Theologians distinguish between the apophatic (what is beyond words) and the kataphatic that can be verbalized.[11] In life, we discover meanings according to one's own experience. Catholic youth learn to struggle with the mystery of the Trinity, Muslim youth with the Prophet's visions, Buddhists with the various traditions extant in the Far East. Those raised in secular societies have a secular horizon bereft of the supernatural. A person's horizon can expand, but what we do not know beckons us toward mystery. Few persons can appropriate their consciousness so as to reach a mystical state. In our day, many Westerners are turning to Zen so as to get hints of the mystical. Zen Buddhists refer to an ultimate mystical experience as *realizing* that "emptiness" which, in fact, means that holistic fullness is a whole greater than its parts. Zen and other mystical paths lead to God; they take us beyond "things" so as to lead to one's being grasped by Ultimate Mind. A mystical state is a simplified mental activity that slows down the thinking process but intensifies consciousness. One begins to pay less attention to bodily sensations or daydreams so as to become fully silent inside.[12]

We have argued that the touchstone of a relevant lived experience lies in our ability to bridge our solitary world within the cultural contexts of the world around us. Each one of us has his/her own life narrative which remains a deeply personal reality but which can also be shared with others despite the possibility of misunderstanding caused by ethnocentrism, ideological self-interest, personal biases or prejudices. This is true not only for the personal experience of individuals but also for that of families, communities or nations. Such experiences occur in cultural situations and historical contexts. It is up to all of us to discern, interrelate and mediate such uniquely personal standpoints affecting communities.

Historical Contexts on Spiritualities That Can Help Unite Humanity in Our Glocal Age

Let us discern what Frederick Douglass said in a series of dialogues he had in 1855 with white slave-owners who could not, would not, grant that slavery is morally wrong. Douglass later wrote that "it is easier to build strong children than to repair broken men."[13] It is in that spirit that we have been striving to link people's lives with God's love. Each one has his/her lived experience, a deeply personal reality that can be partially shared with others. Humans have oppressed and still oppress others in a variety of ways. Lest Christians be oppressors, we have invoked liberation theology, and referred to a communal project in Kenya and to SSC's intimacy-enabling actions—all of which exemplify how we can defuse marginalization and oppression. Christians are called to redress unjust situations.

Another facet of modern life is that overspecialization has led to a loss of wholeness in life that must be recaptured. Formerly, community rituals connected people to the cosmos as they celebrated the changing of the seasons. Today, basic spiritual communities can help us recapture our bondedness with all and live the faith today. The laity can play active roles in proclaiming the Gospel message. Pope Francis has promoted the vision of the Vatican II document *The Church in the Modern World* which helps us understand how the People of God should participate in the Church's mission, how Christians should express the faith of the Church in everyday life. Vatican II's "Decree on the Apostolate of the Laity" recognizes the indispensable role of the laity in evangelizing today. St. Thomas More was one shining example in past centuries. Lay persons come in direct contact with the nitty-gritty of life. Rather than being fixated on hierarchy in the Church, the Pilgrim Church on earth, should focus on needed informal, flexible initiatives. Such movements as *Focolare* (founded by Chiara Lubich and Igino Giordani) and Sant' Egidio have motivated Catholics to get more involved in communal fashion in the problems of the world. They have undertaken many initiatives which can help heal much in our broken world.

We live in a transitional age affected by ongoing political and technical revolutions. With Pope Francis, we are concerned about people's deeper needs. In an interdependent world, what benefits one nation may harm others. We have contextualized political issues so as to bring out the spiritual dimensions relevant to globalization. We did so with a view to help guide people through the mazes of economic inequalities, migrations,[14] and technological breakthroughs. Since the world today still lacks a glocal spirituality that can unite rather than divide humanity, it is important to recall the common roots of the three monotheistic religions, Judaism, Christianity and Islam which often oppose one another. The three also have "in-house" problems with fundamentalist versions. Some Westerners are attracted to Eastern religions because they reject monotheistic traditions for being patriarchal and exclusive. Here again the faith-belief distinction is crucial. Faith unites, beliefs tend to divide adherents of religion.[15] Philosophers and scientists who reject religion also have beliefs. It is important to understand the implications of true faith which are expressed in variable beliefs. On the basis of the Church's time-proven bridging-building ability and of a pressing need for a spirituality that could help unite humanity, we endorse Pope Francis' renewed stress on Church teachings on social justice and new forms of Church ministries that would broaden the roles for the laity in the Church. Jesus' teachings on social justice should be reapplied in every generation after due reflection so as to help Christians live in just ways. Vatican II opened new paths for lay ministries so as to help the Church better sow the seeds of justice. New roles for the laity would complement and enrich the Church's traditional diocesan-parochial structures. Renewed forms of ministries would seem to be crucial to the Church's larger mission of helping unite humanity by promoting a just peace. We have stressed that the history of the Church has been marked by conflict as well as by the deeds of the saints. Saints are those who responded to the challenges facing the Church internally and externally. In the first 800 years of its existence, the Church had to deal with tribes, many of which it converted. Gradually, it had to address many threats to Church unity through a careful process of dogmatic definitions. Beginning with the 16th century, the Church undertook a Counter Reformation. It was not spared the moral dilemmas that stemmed from the colonialist period from the 16th to the 20th centuries. New problems have beset humanity since the Industrial Revolution, including those of the rich-poor divide and environmental issues that flow from the ever greater influence of globalization. The Church, too, must continue to update its perspectives on such issues.

Many areas of life in all parts of the globe are crippled by rampant corruption. Too many politicians the world over receive bribes and work for the highest bidder. Every day, the news makes it clear how difficult it is for those with principles and ideals to achieve their laudable goals. Fortunately, there are many people of good will, among which there are young idealists and those involved in non-profit organizations. It is a "mixed bag" because change is constantly occurring in all areas of life.

Perspectives on New Forms of Ministry in the Face of a Resurgent Authoritarianism

The decline in priestly and religious vocations indicates that the Church must adapt itself to our modern, pluralistic, society. In past ages Catholics lived in self-contained communities which viewed the roles of the priest and nun as integral to their life as Catholic. In most parts of the world Catholics now live in secular societies and the sense of "vocation" can take many new forms other than that of priest or nun. Many of our youth now seek a spiritual identity broader than that defined by "Catholic." They would like to bridge the apparent difficulties of dialoguing, for instance, with Buddhism through time-tested spiritual disciplines. Another task facing the Church is that it must help our youth discern how the Christian faith can be compatible with sound eastern spiritual paths. A further issue is that today, Catholicism has lost some of its credibility due its failure to effectively integrate women into its leadership and ministries. The growing call of women to reverse this failure and the arguments for a married priesthood are other challenges facing the Church today. Many men and women theologians have argued that the Church should at least permit qualified women to become deacons. SCC's are providing new contexts in which the Church can redefine the nature of ministry by incorporating both single and married men and women as liturgical and community leaders and facilitators. If new paradigms[16] of ministry were developed further, these could help solve the crisis in priestly ministry now facing the Church in many parts of the world. There is a need to devise various types of specialized ministries relevant to the secular and ecumenical culture of the 21st century.

Nicholas Obiero cautions that we risk rejecting love unless we be as vulnerable Jesus was. Referring to *Hebrews* 2:9, Obiero writes: "We see in Jesus one who is now crowned with glory and splendor because he submitted to death; by God's grace he had to experience death for all mankind. . . .. We cannot understand others if we do not risk becoming vulnerable. Becoming vulnerable is the beginning of understanding others. It is the beginning of that sense of wonder of our unrestricted desire to know the truth, the moment when things begin to happen."[17] It is part of the Christian mystery that with Christ we must become vulnerable, empty ourselves to be filled with his grace. Being vulnerable can be contrasted with an article[18] by Lars-Erick Cerman which does not mention Pope Francis, but is one with the pope's views on the decline of the liberal, international world order constructed after WWII. That order, dependent on the United Nations and US/Europe, is now under assault by nationalist[19] and authoritarian leaders such as Trump, Erdogan, Putin, and Bolsonaro. Pope Francis, one of the few world leaders attempting to forge a new unity in the world, needs the support of other religious leaders and institutions to resist growing authoritarianism. It also requires a viable glocal ethics and a deep glocal spirituality—a type of prophetic dialogue open to being vulnerable. In Obiero's words: "Religious love enables us to discover who we are. It makes us realize that being in love with God is a relationship that goes beyond the self. It makes us reach out to the other, to reach out to our neighbors with love and compassion." (Ibid). This is in line with Pope Francis' view that "Each individual Christian and every community is called to be an instrument of God for the liberation and promotion of the poor. . . .. This demands that we be docile and attentive to the cry of the poor and to come to their aid."[20] Mission means that one love one's neighbor as one's self. (Mark 12:31).

Pope Francis: Redefining the Nature of Church's Mission in a World Divided by Conflicts

Pope Francis has linked the ecological crisis with the social imbalance affecting most of the world today:

We must regain the conviction that we need one another, that we have a shared responsibility for others and the world, and that being good and decent are worth it. We have had enough of immorality and the mockery of ethics, goodness, faith and honesty. It is time to acknowledge that light-hearted superficiality has done us no good. When the foundations of social life are corroded, what ensues are battles over conflicting interests, new forms of violence and brutality, and obstacles to the growth of a genuine culture of care for the environment." (*Laudato Si*, 229).

The pope has made it clear that global warming needs to be part of the social justice agenda for Christianity and the world religions. A consumer lifestyle—unsustainable on the planet as a whole—has led to increasing levels of deforestation, pollution of rivers and streams, a rapid decline in biodiversity among living species and increasing suburban sprawl. Trump's withdrawal from the Paris Climate Agreement indicates the increasing isolation of the US among the industrialized nations of the world regarding efforts to control global warming.[21]

The pope, in criticizing climate change doubters, has said that history will judge those who failed to take the necessary decisions to curb the threat of heat-trapping emissions. When asked about climate change and the spate of hurricanes that pummeled the U.S., Mexico and the Caribbean in 2017, he replied: "Those who deny this must go to the scientists and ask them. They speak very clearly," he said, referring to experts who blame global warming on man-made activities. He added that scientists have clearly charted what needs to be done to reverse course on global warming. All, especially politicians have a "moral responsibility" to do their part. "These aren't opinions pulled out of thin air. They are very clear;"[22] then he added that history will judge the political decisions made on this vital topic.

Globalization, Capitalism and Migration

Immigrants from Africa, the Middle East and Latin America and the Western communities hosting them must cope with inherent cultural-religious differences.[23] Many well-to-do Westerners think they have an inalienable right to go settle wherever and whenever they choose (often in secluded areas). The racist-capitalist attitudes of nominally Christian people run betray the Gospel.[24] Pope Francis expressed his concern for migrants and refugees on his very first trip outside of Rome when he visited Lampedusa Island in the Mediterranean where many refugees wanting to migrate to

Europe are being held. He lamented the fate of the thousands who have died at sea. He posed the question God had put to Cain: "Where is your brother?" Globalization has led to growth of slums worldwide. Some cities are now fragmented along the lines of religious affiliation. The growing populism and hostility to migrants in recent times suggest that a mission spirituality should closely examine recent changes in the world's cultural contexts. The Church is called to minister to such problems afflicting the world.

We now live in fluid, dynamic cultural contexts due to the emergence of new economic and cultural structures that transcend national boundaries. Many U. S. jobs have been outsourced to other countries. Ever less automobiles, electronic goods such as cell phones, computers, entertainment devices and clothes are still manufactured in the U. S. On the other hand, the migration of peoples from Asia, Africa and Latin America in search of employment in the urbanized nations of Europe and the USA are also part of the fabric of our time. Many immigrants live in utter poverty or are forced to take very low wage jobs and live in subhuman conditions in segregated sectors of society. The income and cultural gap between the highly educated and technologically-proficient elites[25] and the immigrants seeking employment or fleeing violence has accelerated in many parts of the world. The social justice teachings of the Church and the 1990 UN Declaration on Human Rights both address such issues. The latter calls for the "Protection of the Rights of All Migrant Workers and Members of Their Families and Non-Citizens." It clarifies the rights of groups such as migrant workers who live in a nation for extended time periods but are not citizens of the country where they work. Article 7 would protect the rights of migrant workers and their families regardless of "sex, race, color, language, religion or conviction, . . . ethnic or social origin or other status."[26] It also insists on the basic rights of migratory workers and their families even if they lack legal status. Many migrant workers in the US were raised in a Catholic culture. The Church is often the only institutional refuge for many of these migrant workers. Pope Francis has consistently addressed the Church's role in welcoming and protecting refugees and immigrants. His 2018 statement for the World Day of Immigrants and Refugees highlighted his concern for those who have often been marginalized or excluded due to poverty, violence or warfare in their country of origin.

American and Church Ideals: Their Ambiguous Nature

One of America's ideals is "Give me your tired, your poor, your huddled masses yearning to breathe free," emblazoned on the base of the Statue of Liberty. Taken from one of Emma Lazarus' poems, it epitomizes the challenges facing America. As a Jewish American woman, Lazarus faced the challenge of belonging to two often conflicting worlds. Her celebrating the "other," conveyed her deep loyalty to America and Judaism. How assimilate the millions of immigrants wanting to live in freedom? The U.S. Immigration and Customs Enforcement agency has had its share of questionable practices. Foreign students coming to the USA from regions engulfed in violence should be welcomed. Some of these will be part of the next generation of world leaders. The educational system of the U. S is one of its great strengths. More scholarships are needed for youth from developing areas of the world. The US pioneering efforts in educating immigrants are laudable—an example of a "legitimate freedom" of action. Uncertainty about the world's "hot spots" should not deter us from generously interacting with their people. Likewise, evangelical ideals should motivate the universal Church. In our time of crises and of new opportunities, the Church must make its domestic policies more pastoral if it hopes to be taken seriously. It has sometimes remained silent in the face of violations of human rights by its own priests and bishops as in the case of the recent sexual scandals that have engulfed the Church. As to the alleged silence of the Church during the holocaust, Pope Francis has announced that the Vatican will release the secret archives of Pope Pius XII in March of 2020 to resolve any question of the Church's complicity.

Global Capitalism's Moral Decay and Creation Spirituality's Countervailing Efforts

The failure of Christians to challenge the moral decay of business practices must be evaluated through the eyes of the Church's teaching on social justice. Many of the executives of global corporations are "practicing Christians." In fact, their behavior often lacks ethical integrity. According to Jeffrey Sachs of the Earth Institute, Columbia University, global capitalism initially motivated European conquerors. It unleashed both greed and addictions — the hunger for sugar reinforced the plantation slave system in the Americas. Sachs admits that as an economist, he was never formally schooled in ethics, a lack that permeates practitioners of his craft. The pope, by warning us that global capitalism is "putting us in profound peril," has emerged "as the most important person on the planet."[27] Since Pope Leo XIII's 1891 *Rerum Novarum*, the Church has warned against capitalist excesses. Pope Francis stresses that the global capitalist system[28] oppresses the poor and threatens life on the planet. In faulting Donald Trump for subverting the Paris Accords on climate change, the pope is asking Christians to join others in taking action. Countries with large reserves of oil and gas now have great leverage. Due to global warming, these sources of energy must be supplanted by renewable sources such as solar, wind and geothermal power. Al Gore's "An Inconvenient Truth" and the Peace and Justice Summit have led to cooperation in this area. Many young people want to join these efforts, but some view Christian theologies as obstacles to ecological activism. The Creation Spirituality of Matthew Fox, Thomas Berry and Diarmuid O'Murchu, as well as Pope Francis' *Laudato Si*, are all meant to remedy shortcomings in this area.

Toward Overcoming Religious Intolerance and Unbelief through Needed Cooperation

Another global development demanding our attention after 9/11 is the growth of terrorist attacks and the rise of Islamic and Christian and fundamentalism. The latter, largely centered in the United States, has been influential in misguiding US foreign policy. Islamic fundamentalism, originally based Afghanistan and Pakistan, has recently infiltrated some European and African countries. Because the Catholic Church is present in both the US and the Middle East, it has the potential to mediate Christian-Islamic differences in several ways. The Church's Peace and Justice tradition is matched by Islam's stress on social welfare for the poor, the oppressed and the mentally or physically disabled. Christianity and Islam both pioneered the development of health care in the Middle Ages when they collaborated in founding the first university-based medical schools of the West. All three religions of the Book drew extensively from the Greek philosophical and scientific traditions in the formative scientific period of the early Middle Ages. Much of the Western curriculum in medicine and the natural sciences have Muslim antecedents that were translated from Arabic into Latin in the 11th and 12th centuries. The *Koran* (4:58) teaches that justice must be practiced by all: "And when ye judge between man and man, judge justly." Muslims are expected to donate a percentage of their assets to charities caring for the poor, widows and the disabled. Muslims intellectuals provided the rationale to ensure that all, including the poor and the mentally impaired receive needed medical care. If fundamentalist Christian missionaries sometimes cause problems due to their failure to understand the deeper aspects of beliefs, learning compassion would help them overcome the intolerance that pits fundamentalists of divergent traditions against one another. Domestic and foreign relief projects to deal with the flood of refugees from the Middle East and Africa should help us realize that all share a common humanity. No one is immune from possible tragedy. By responding to human crises, we awaken the deeper dimensions of our conscience and transform our own self-understanding—a lesson Pope Francis learned early in life.

Sadly, the rise of skepticism about the truths of religion initiated by Descartes due to his rejection of the scholastic method was exacerbated by the Wars of Religion in Europe in the 16th and 17th centuries. The Enlightenment philosophers wanted to replace the personal God of revelation with an impersonal power that had created the universe but then left it to its devices—with humans as caretakers of the earth. Catholicism and Islam have both rejected the Enlightenment's "autonomous self," but they have not yet effectively bridged the growing gaps between the natural sciences and theology. Pope Francis has delineated their complementarity. His *Laudato Si* cites areas[29] where the two should collaborate such as in medical science and technology. The Church serves as a counterweight to religious intolerance. Jesus' death on the cross heals our broken world. The bravest of his disciples have witnessed to him even to the point of death. Violent terrorism spawned by fundamentalism haunt our world. Both Buddhism and Christianity warn us of self-love. Healing a broken world demands justice and a sound spirituality. Buddhism promotes an ethic of compassion for all living beings. The Dalai Lama has been one of the most articulate spokespersons for a global ethic that can help unite rather than divide humanity. Hopefully, world institutions will develop and implement a glocally-morally coherent world view devoted to respecting human rights and to promoting sustainable development, economic justice and global peace.

By Way of Conclusion

Jesus charged the Church to preach the Good News to all. The Church has done much to address social problems—but often belatedly. Theologians and bishops are not immune from biases nor the pressures of others. Pope Francis asks Church leaders to bridge our human divides. His is a moral voice that seeks to redirect the political and economic spheres in just ways for the benefit of all— especially of victims and of the poor. A profound, challenging intimation of Christ's Good News is well expressed by Richard Rohr:

"What if Christ is a name for the immense spaciousness of all true Love?
What if Christ refers to an infinite horizon that pulls us both from within and pulls us forward, too?
What if Christ is another name for every thing in its fullness?"[30]

Rohr's is a Christocentric vision which parallels the pope's glocal vision. It represents a new spirituality[31] growing in popularity. His Christic typology corresponds in many ways to our own overall interpretation of Pope Francis' ministry, his visionary appeals to reform the Church by going back to the teachings of Jesus. Implied in this process are urgent calls on society to shed its prejudices, welcome migrants, and correctly reassess the complex, comprehensive implications of all reality by radically re-conceptualizing nature's potentialities and our roles as stewards of God's creation.

Notes

1 Isaiah 2: 1-4 foretold that in the new messianic era Yahweh's prophetic word would go forth from Jerusalem to all the nations. The early Christians thought of Pentecost as the fulfillment of Isaiah's prophecy. "Word of God" 'in the Acts of the Apostles refers to the Church's missionary expansion from Jerusalem to Rome. The expansion was due to divine intervention. See Gerald Grudzen, *Genesis of the Christian Experience*, Diakonia Press, 1973.
2 www.ansa.it/english/news/vatican/2019/01/17/gods-word-not-ideology-says-pope_c8a2ccf0-f6f9-4795-95d3-635e82731844.html Francis added :"This is what the lukewarm are like: those who always compromise. We, too, often do this. Even when the Lord lets us know the path, even with the commandments, also with the inspiration of the Holy Spirit, but I prefer something else, and I try to find a way to go down two tracks, limping on both legs."
3 Even criminals are glocally organized: https://onlinelibrary.wiley.com/doi/pdf/10.1111/1468-2311.00109
4 https://creativesystemsthinking.wordpress.com/2015/10/24/realize-you-are-the-earth-thich-nhat-hanh/
5 Douglas Hofstader's *Godel, Escher, Bach* used the works of these brilliant pioneers to illustrate what he meant by "strange loop" or "tangled hierarchy." Although he goes into many details to show how physical processes generate minds and meaning, arguing that loops at the level of electrons and quarks, give rise to loops at the level of

132 Chapter 9

biology, genes and neurons, even of symbols meaning, he has little to say about good and evil.

6 The pope warned "gangsters that they will go to hell unless they repent and stop doing evil. www. bbc.com/ news/av/world-europe-26695549/pope-francis-denounces-evil-blood-stained-mafia. On the other hand, he likes J.R.R. Tolkien and has read his works. He particularly grew fond of Frodo and Bilbo whom he used as examples of hopeful heroes called to walk a path in the unfolding drama between good and evil.

7 Bernard Lonergan, *Method in Theology*, 115.

8 Frederic Martel has written on gays in the Vatican. As to this issue and/or the problem of sexual abuse by priests worldwide *National Catholic Reporter*, Feb. 22-March 7,2019,) the pope said: "We must not get scandalized over this. They are steps in a process." Presumably, he is reacting in a similar way re the gay problem in the Vatican.

9 See, for instance, Casey Boodt, Leendert Mos, "Hermeneutics of Lived Experience: The Foundations of a Historical Psychology," *Recent Trends in Theoretical Psychology*, 1993, 111-22, on today's foundationalist crises.

10 In *Method in Theology*, 236, Lonergan explores cultural changes. A believer is afloat on a sea of multiplying theologies, without rudder or compass. There are things that concern others but in which one is not interested. The extent of one's interests fix a horizon within which one is confined. The confinement may result from the historical tradition within which one is born, from the limitations of one's social milieu, from one one's psychological aptitudes. But one may also reconsider present limiting conditions—as Pope Francis has been asking us to do.

11 Phil Mc Shane, in a private message note on Lonergan's *Method*, 355, says that "The flaw in religious prayer patterns is the failure of some effective sub-population to rise to the being-with-God that is kataphatic reaching. This leaves us in a commonsense wishful helplessness that, of course, can be Quiet but with 'no fruit to be borne.'"

12 Robert Forman, "What does Mysticism have to Teach us about Consciousness," The Second Tucson Conference. April, 1996 https://books.google.de/books?id=dliyExsqYGwC&printsec=frontcover#v=onepage&q&f=false. Such a silence is a pure consciousness event (PCE) experienced by mystics of many religions. As heightened cognizance, PCE's are "a perceived unity of one's own awareness per se with the objects around one, an immediate sense of a quasi-physical unity between self, objects and other people, ...(what may be called a)

unitive mystical state." They may well be the E. coli of consciousness studies, the least complex encounter with awareness per se sought by students of consciousness. Dogen, Eckhart, al-Hallaj were all apophatic mystics; one may not be aware of a specific thought, but something persists in such a PCE, a contentless consciousness, known in Zen as *sunyata*—a "void." William Johnston in *Silent Music*, (New York: Harper & Row, 1974), speaks of an imagistically filling (kataphatic) mysticism and an emptying (apophatic) one; the latter is devoid of the sensory language used in the former.

13 *Frederick Douglass Quotes*, www.brainyquote.com/authors/frederick_douglass

14 Catholic immigrants into the USA today mirror, in some ways, the socioeconomic group attracted to Christianity in the first three centuries of its existence. This involved an informal evangelization process brought about by the influence of marginalized people who migrated from Jerusalem to other Mediterranean areas in 70, CE. Scattered from their base in Jerusalem, they went about spreading the good news which had brought them joy, release, and a new life. They went with the conviction of those not paid to say that sort of thing. This is why they were taken seriously: the movement spread mostly among the lower classes. (Bevans and Schroeder: *Constants*, 86).

15 The faith-belief distinction is crucial. Faith links us to God, beliefs are potentially divisive interpretations. We Christians must seek the proper balance between individuals and groups. A glocal-eye discerns the proper balance—not that of evasive, (often silent) bourgeois beliefs but of a silent, alert faith pregnant with the holy, with truth.

16 There is no single paradigm to fit all cases. Communities must experientially probe their actual situation.

17 Nicholas Obiero, *Towards a Theology of Mission and Evangelization in Kenya in a Post-Colonial Context: Challenges and Opportunities*. PhD Thesis, Toronto St. Michael's College. 2017, 182-83.

18 Lars-Erik Cederman, "Blood for Soil: The Fatal Temptations of Ethnic Politics" www.foreignaffairs.com/articles/ 2019-02-12/blood-soil

19 Pope Francis on Jan. 7, 2019, told diplomats that a resurgent nationalism threatens peace (*La Croix*, Jan. 8, '19).

20 http://www.vatican.va/evangelii-gaudium/en/files/assets/basic-html/page147.html

21 When Trump met the Pope at the Vatican in 2017, he received a copy of *Laudato Si*. A very ironic papal gesture!

22 Associated Press, September 11, 2017. www.gq.com/story/the-pope-is-fed-up-with-climate-change-deniers

23 In a message for the 105th World Day of Migrants and Refugees (27 May 2019) Pope Francis urged "society to drop its prejudice towards migrants. The migration issue is not just about migrants and refugees, but it is also about our fears. It is not just about migrants." Referring to the signs of meanness we see around us, he added that "The problem is not that we have doubts and fear. The problem is when they condition our way of thinking and acting to the point of making us intolerant, closed and perhaps even - without realizing it - racist."

24 For the pope, poverty is morally superior to a selfish, predatory oligarchy—oligarchs are destroying our society and the planet; by exploiting labor and nature, they provoke economic inequalities. "Judging the economy with the measure of GDP does not take into account things" that reduce our well-being like environmental degradation and violence. Purchasing power and political power should not be concentrated in the hands of a few. Oligarchy erodes the mutual trust and affection without which a society cannot function happily or well. See Truthout.org/ articles/oligarchy-is-destroying-our-society-and-the-planet. Jan 24, 2017. The moral bankruptcy of capitalism is cynically expressed by JPMorgan Chase CEO Jamie Dimon. He claims that socialism would be "a disaster for our country." JPMorgan under Dimon received a $25bn socialist-like bailout in 2008.

25 In *Laudato Si*, 149, Pope Francis exposes the dangers of the technological paradigm ruling our lives.

26 https://www.ohchr.org/en/professionalinterest/pages/cmw.aspx

27 www.ncronline.org/news/environment/pope-francis-blunt-critique-capitalism-praised-needed-warning (2018). Sachs explained how free market deregulation leads to people's dying because of company practices. One CEO replied: "That's just the way our system works." Concern for the human consequences is simply factored out.

28 In 1998, when still an archbishop, the pope wrote a book, an entire chapter of which focused on "the limits of capitalism." He wrote it after then-Pope John Paul II visited Fidel Castro in Cuba. In a chapter on economics, the future pope argued that capitalism can be good for development, but, lacking morals, it promotes selfish behavior.

29 In response to *Laudato Si*, some US dioceses are committed to help shape the future of our planet. Bishop Oscar Cantu of San Jose, CA, and Marita Grudzen, Chair of the Diocesan Environmental Commission,

are focusing on Care for Creation projects do to so.
30 https://cac.org/another-name-for-every-thing-the-universal-christ/ Yet, we ask whether and how the notion of "the Remnant" in the Old Testament might take on new meaning; it needs new applications in our secularized age.
31 Rohr's Christic spirituality is an alternative to an eclecticism that uncritically dabbles with Eastern religions.

SELECTED BIBLIOGRAPHY

Aman, Kenneth. "Fighting for God: the Military and Religion in Chile," www.jstor.org/stable/24459104

Andraos, Michel. *The Church and Indigenous Peoples in the Americas: In Between Reconciliation and Decolonization* Eugene OR: Cascade Books, 2019.

Arendt, Hannah. *The Origins of Totalitarianism*. Orlando, FL: Harcourt, 1968.

Bevans, Stephen B. and Roger P. Schroeder. *Constants in Context: A Theology of Mission for Today*. New York: Orbis, 2004.

—. *Prophetic Dialogue*, New York, Orbis, 2011.

Bulliet, Richard W. *The Case for Islamo-Christian Civilization*. NY: Columbia University Press, 2004.

Carroll, James. "Two Scenes from Pope Francis's Revolution of Tenderness," May 1, 2017. www.newyorker.com/news/news-desk/two-scenes-from-pope-franciss-revolution-of-tenderness

Carson, Rachel. *Silent Spring*. New York: Houghton, Mifflin, 1962.

Carter, Stephen L., *Culture of Disbelief*. New York: Harper, 1993.

Costello, Stephen J. *Hermeneutics and the Psychoanalysis of Religion*. Oxford: Peter Lang, 2010.

De Lubac, Henri Cardinal. *The Religion of Teilhard de Chardin*. New York: Image Books,1967.

Francis, Pope. "Address to Fraternity Conference," www.vaticannews.va/en/pope/news/2019-02/pope-francis-uae-global-conference-human-fraternity-full-text.html

—. *The Joy of the Gospel*, Vatican City, 2013.

—. *Laudato Si*. Vatican City. May, 2005.

—. "Message for the 105th World Day of Migrants and Refugees," 27 May 2019.

—. *Praedicate Evangelium*. Draft of, https://www.ncronline.org/news/opinion/francis-draft-curial-reform-fundamentally-reimagines-vaticans-role

Freeman, Laurence, OSB. "Some Reflections on the Rule of St Benedict: Four Principles or Attitudes, *Via Vitae*. January 2006.

Freire, Paulo. *Pedagogy of the Oppressed*. NY: Seabury, 1970.

Friedman, Thomas. *The World Is Flat: A Brief History of the Twenty-first Century*. Farrar, Straus and Giroux, 2005.

Gichuhi, George N. *The Spirituality of Small Christian Communities in Eastern Africa*. Eldoret, Kenya: Gaba 1985.

Grassi Joseph, *A World to Win: The Missionary Methods of Paul the Apostle*. NY: Orbis, 1965.

Grudzen, Gerald. *Burying the Sword: Confronting Jihadism with Interfaith Education*. Author House. 2017

—. "The Divine Imprint in Nature: Fethullah Gulen and Teilhard de Chardin." *Omega: The Indian Journal of Science and Religion*   s. December, 2016.

—. *Medical Theory About the Body and Soul in the Middle Ages: The First Western Medical Curriculum at Monte Cassino*. Lewiston, NY: Mellen Press, 2007.

Guttierez, Gustavo. Revised introduction to *A Theology of Liberation*. NY: Orbis, 1988.

Hart, Patrick, Jonathan Montaldo, *The Intimate Merton: His Life from His Journals.*HarperOne, 2001.
Healey, Joselph and Jeanne Hinton, *Small Christian Communities Today.* N. Y. Orbis, 2005.
Helminiak, Daniel. *Brain, Consciousness, and God.* State of New York, Univ. Press, 2015.
Huntington, Samuel. *The Clash of Civilization: Remaking of the World Order.* Simon and Schuster, 1996.
Ji-Sun Kim, Grace. "Five Asian concepts that can deepen our understanding of the Holy Spirit." https://sojo.net/biography/grace-ji-sun-kim 12-28-2018.
John Paul II, Pope. *Gift and Mystery.* New York: Image Books, 1996.
—. *Redemptoris Missio.* Washington, D.C.: United States Catholic Conference, 1991.
Judd, Stephen P. "The Indigenous Theology Movement in Latin America," in *Resurgent Voices in Latin America*, edited by Edward L. Cleary and Timothy J. Steigenga. Rutgers Univ. Press, 2004 210-30.
Kearney, Richard. *Anatheism: Returning to God After God.* Columbia Univ., 2009.
King, Ursula. Spirit of Fire: *The Life and Vision of Teilhard de Chardin.* Brill, NV: 1996.
—. *Teilhard de Chardin and Eastern Religions.* New York: Paulist Press, 2011.
Knitter, Paul. *Without Buddha I Could Not Be a Christian.* Oneworld Publications, 2013.
Lencioni, Joe. "Total Kenosis, True Sunyata, and the Plerotic Self of Thomas Merton and Masao Abe in *The Journal of Theta Alpha Kappa*, Vol. 30, No. 1, Spring 2006.
Lonergan, Bernard. *A Second Collection.* London: Darton, Longman, & Todd, 1974.
—. "Healing and Creating in History" in *A Third Collection*, ed. B Fred Crowe. New York: Paulist Press, 1985.
—. Insight: *A Study of Human Understanding, Collected Works*, vol. 3, ed. Frederick Crowe and Robert Doran. Toronto: University of Toronto Press, 1992.
—. *Method in Theology.* New York: Seabury, 1972.
Merton, Thomas. *Conjectures of a Guilty Bystander.* New York: Doubleday, 1968.
— *No Man is an Island.* New York: Harcourt, 1955.
Moltmann, Jürgen. *The Church in the Power of the Spirit: A Contribution to Messianic Ecclesiology.* Fortress, 1993.
Mother Teresa: *In my Own Words.* Edited by Jose Luis Gonzales-Balado. New York: Gramercy, 1996.
Obiero, Nicholas. *Towards a Theology of Mission and Evangelization in Kenya in a Post-Colonial Context: Challenges and Opportunities.* PhD Thesis, Toronto St. Michael's College. 2017.
Okumura, Ichiro. *Awakening to Prayer.* Washington, D.C.: Institute of Carmelite Studies, 1974.
Orobator, A. E. *Religion and Faith in African: Confessions of an Animist.* Orbis: 2018.
Pagels, Elaine. "Women in the Early Church," www.pbs.org/wgbh/pages/frontline/shows/ religion/ first/roles.html
Raymaker, John. *Bernard Lonergan's Third Way of the Heart and Mind: Bridging Some Buddhist-Christian-Muslim-Secularist Misunderstandings with a Global Secularity Ethics.* Lanham: Hamilton, 2016.

— with Ijaz Durrani. *Empowering Climate-Change Strategies with Bernard Lonergan's Method*. Lanham, MD: UPA, 2015.

Roberts, Bob Jr., *Transformation: How Glocal Churches Transform Lives and the World*. Zondervan, 2006.

Rohr, Richard. *The Universal Christ, How a Forgotten Reality Can Change Everything We See*. Convergent, 2019.

Romero, Jorge. "Don Quixote Rides Again: Illusion and Delusion in Conrad's Lord Jim." www.clas.ufl.edu /ipsa/2005/proc/romero.pdf

Roudometof, Victor. *Glocalization: A Critical Introduction*. New York: Routledge, 2016.

Teilhard de Chardin. *Building the Earth*. 1969. https://www.azquotes.com/quote/690346

—. "Hymn of the Universe. The Mass on the World." www.stmchapelhill.org/documents/

—. " *La parole attendue*" In *Cahiers Pierre Teilhard de Chardin*. Vol. 4, 22-29. Paris: Desclee. 1963.

—. *The Making of a Mind*. Translated by Rene Hague. New York, Harper and Row. 1965.

—. *The Divine Milieu*. Translated by B. Wall, A Dru, N Lindsay, D. MacKinnon. New York: Harper & Row. 1960.

Thorbjørnsen, PVW. *A Christian Vedanta? Bede Griffiths and the Hindu-Christian Encounter*. https://www.duo.uio.no/handle/10852/24026

INDEX

A
Al-Ghazali, 60, 70
Anatheism, 29
Apophatic-Kataphatic, 29, 30,
Aquinas, Thomas St., 121
Atheism, 15, 21, 22, 30
Augustine, St., 13

B
Benedict, Saint, 12-14
Bevans, Stephen, 7, 8 17, 60
Buddhism, 51, 59, 71,102
Building Bridges, 3, 55, 63

C
Carson, Rachel, 3, 38
Carter, Stephen L., 29
Catherine of Siena, St., 22
Centering Prayer, 30
Christian-Islamic Dialogue, 38
Climate Crises, 3, 39
Constantine, Emperor, 5, 15, 16
Coptic Church, 66

D
Dalai Lama, 71, 99, 130
De Lubac, Henri, 42

E
Ethics, its Essential Roles, 125

F
Fox, Matthew, 129
Francis of Assisi, St, vii, 51, 57

Freire, Paulo, 64, 107

G
Glocal, Importance of, 4, 21, 42, 51, 120. passim
Gospels, 4. 120
Griffiths, Bede, 58, 97
Grudzen, Gerald, 69, 136
Grudzen, Marita, 79, 135
Gulen, Fethullah, 38, 69
Guttierez, Gustavo, 88

H
Healey, Joseph. 108, 115
Helminiak, Daniel, 52
Hildegard, Saint, 12
Houston, Jean, 51, 65

I
Inculturation, 8, 26
Islam, 50, 55

J
Jeong, 95, 96, 100
Ji-Sun Kim, Grace, 95
Judd, Steven, 9

K
Kasper, Walter, Cardinal ,25
Kearney, Richard, 29
King, Ursula , 43, 46,141, 142

L
Laudato Si, Encyclical, vii, 33, 67,

142 Index

134, passim
Lonergan, Bernard, 32, 68, 93

M
Marx, Karl, 21, 99
Mercy, Importance of, 8, 24, 25
Merton, Thomas, 9, 55, 98, 102
Mother Teresa, St., 24, 31
Muhammad, Prophet, 51, 55

O
Obiero, Nicholas, 125
Omega Point, 35

P
Pontiff, Pontifex, 4, 5
Poole, Steven, 29
Pope Benedict XVI, 53, 117
Pope Gregory VII, 19
Pope Pius XII, 128
Pope St. John XXIII, 5, 8, 63
Pope St. John Paul II, viii, 37, 43
Pope Leo XIII, 128

Q
Quevedo, Cardina 61
Qur'an, (Koran) 55, 129

R
Rahner, Karl, 33
Raymaker, John, 64, 69, 93
Ricci, Matteo, 96, 97
Ricoeur, Paul, 22, 29, 30

Rohr, Richard, 37, 130, 131
Romero, Oscar St, 32, 105, 107

S
Saint Paul, 50, 51, 64
Sant' Egidio, 8, 122
Schroeder, Roger, 7, 8, 17, 60
Schweitzer, Albert, 3, 4
Small Christian Communities (SSC's), 105-107, 116
Spiritualities, Roles of, 122
Sufism , 38, 40, 55, 56, 69, 82
Suzuki, D. T., 101
Synods, 23, 31, 62, 88, 91, 92

T
Teasdale, Wayne, 27
Teilhard de Chardin, Pierre, 33-42, 52
Thich Nhat Hanh, 120
Transformative Changes, 15, 38, 60, 61, 77, 89, 110

U
Underhill, Evelyn, 52

V
Vatican II Council, 4, 5, 9, 98
Vision, Visionary, 34, 36, 37, 61, 122, 131

Z
Zen, 56, 98, 99, 120, 122, 130

www.ingramcontent.com/pod-product-compliance
Lightning Source LLC
Chambersburg PA
CBHW022015300426
44117CB00005B/204